TOP

MEDITERRANEAN DIET
COOKBOOK FOR BEGINNERS

1800 Days Classic & Innovative Recipe Books to Indulge in a Mediterranean Culinary Adventure and Stay Healthy Everyday | Stress-Free 4-Week Meal Plan

Deb T. Johnson

CONTENTS

Fish And Seafood Recipes 17

Poultry And Meats Recipes 28

Beans , Grains, And Pastas Recipes 64

Fruits, Desserts And Snacks Recipes 76

Appendix : Recipes Index 85

INTRODUCTION

Journey Beyond Borders with Deb T. Johnson's Mediterranean Masterpiece. Close your eyes for a moment and imagine a sunlit scene: tables laden with platters of glistening olives, fish caught fresh from sapphire waters, golden olive oil drizzled over crisp salads, and vine-ripened tomatoes bursting with flavor. Welcome to the Mediterranean, a region not just known for its picturesque landscapes but more so for a culinary heritage that has tantalized and nourished souls for millennia.

In the heart of this tradition stands Deb T. Johnson, your culinary guide to this beautiful part of the world. As you turn the pages of this Mediterranean Diet cookbook, you won't just find recipes—you'll embark on a voyage. With each dish, Deb unravels a story, a legacy, and a passion handed down through generations. Her meticulous curation is not just about flavor; it's an ode to a way of life where food is a celebration, a daily ritual of love, and an emblem of health.

Having journeyed through coastal villages, bustling Mediterranean markets, and tranquil olive groves, Deb brings to you a tapestry of dishes that are as diverse as they are unified in their health benefits. The Mediterranean diet, revered globally by nutritionists and doctors, isn't just another trend—it's a testament to time, a tried and true lifestyle that promotes longevity, wellness, and, above all, the joy of good food.

For those unfamiliar with the diet's heart-healthy pulses, the invigorating crunch of its fresh produce, or the rich flavors of its extra virgin olive oils, Deb eases the path with clear, step-by-step instructions and insightful anecdotes. And for those who have already been seduced by the Mediterranean's culinary charm, she offers a deeper dive, with dishes that'll rekindle memories and flavors.

But this cookbook is more than just a collection of recipes; it's an invitation. An invitation to embrace a diet that has the power to transform, to explore ingredients in their purest form, and to set forth on a gastronomic adventure like no other. Let Deb T. Johnson whisk you away on a culinary journey, where the aroma of fresh herbs fills the air, and every bite is a dance of flavors on your palate.

Dive in, explore, cook, and celebrate the Mediterranean's best-kept secrets with fervor and zest. Bon Appétit!

Sources of the Mediterranean Diet

The Mediterranean Diet, inspired by the traditional dietary patterns of countries bordering the Mediterranean Sea, is renowned for its numerous health benefits. Central to this diet is the emphasis on fresh, seasonal, and locally-sourced produce, with fruits and vegetables forming the core of daily consumption. These provide essential vitamins, minerals, and fiber integral to overall health.

Whole grains, like bread, pasta, and rice, preferably consumed in their unrefined forms, act as primary energy sources. Legumes such as beans, lentils, and chickpeas contribute protein and fiber, promoting satiety and digestive health. Olive oil, especially extra-virgin, replaces other fats, offering heart-healthy monounsaturated fats and antioxidants.

Fish, rich in omega-3 fatty acids, features prominently, while red meat is limited. Dairy, primarily cheese and yogurt, is consumed in moderation, and nuts and seeds provide additional healthy fats, protein, and essential nutrients. Poultry and eggs offer alternative protein sources, consumed judiciously.

A hallmark of this diet is the use of herbs and spices, like basil, garlic, and rosemary, adding flavor without relying on salt. Wine, typically red, is consumed in moderation, mainly with meals. Sweets, focusing on fruits, honey, and nuts, are occasional treats.

More than just food, the Mediterranean Diet encapsulates a lifestyle. It emphasizes the importance of communal meals, physical activity, and relishing life's pleasures. Its balanced approach, rich in nutrients and low in processed foods, has been linked to longevity, reduced risk of chronic diseases, and improved mental well-being.

What health changes can the Mediterranean Diet bring about?

Heart Health: Multiple studies have shown that the Mediterranean diet can reduce the risk of heart diseases. Its emphasis on olive oil, nuts, and fresh produce means lower levels of unhealthy cholesterol and better overall heart health.

Weight Management: The diet promotes satiety with its high fiber content, leading to reduced calorie intake and aiding weight loss. Moreover, the healthy fats, lean proteins, and complex carbohydrates support weight maintenance.

Mental Health Benefits: Some studies suggest that the Mediterranean diet can help protect against depression and cognitive decline. The omega-3 fatty acids from fish, along with other nutrients, play a role in brain health.

Supports Digestive Health: With its emphasis on whole grains, legumes, fruits, and vegetables, the diet is rich in fiber which promotes healthy digestion and can prevent conditions like constipation.

Bone Health: The Mediterranean diet provides nutrients like calcium and magnesium from dairy products, fish, and greens, supporting bone health and potentially reducing the risk of osteoporosis.

How to get the most out of the Mediterranean Diet recipes?

Maximizing the benefits and enjoyment of a Mediterranean Diet cookbook involves a combination of understanding the diet's principles, staying organized, experimenting, and adapting it to one's personal tastes and needs.

Understand the Basics: Familiarize yourself with the foundational principles of the Mediterranean diet. Knowing the core components, like the emphasis on fruits, vegetables, whole grains, lean proteins, and healthy fats, will help you grasp the essence of recipes and potentially innovate.

Plan Ahead: The 28-Day Meal Plan in the cookbook provides an excellent roadmap. Use it to prepare your weekly grocery list, ensuring you have all necessary ingredients on hand.

Start Simple: Begin with basic recipes to build confidence. As you become more acquainted with Mediterranean flavors and techniques, venture into more complex dishes.

Experiment and Adapt: Everyone's palate is unique. Feel free to adjust recipes based on your preferences. Substitute ingredients, adjust seasoning, or combine elements from different recipes.

Incorporate Local and Seasonal Produce: The Mediterranean diet is all about fresh, local, and seasonal ingredients. Visit local farmers' markets to get the freshest produce, which will enhance the flavors of your dishes.

Pair with the Right Beverage: While water is the mainstay, the Mediterranean diet also welcomes beverages like herbal teas and red wine (in moderation). Learn about wine pairings to complement the flavors of your dishes.

Engage in Social Dining: One of the pillars of the Mediterranean lifestyle is enjoying meals with family and friends. Share the dishes you've made with loved ones, turning mealtime into a joyful, communal experience.

Maintain a Balanced Approach: While the cookbook offers 1800 recipes, it's essential to ensure you're getting a diverse range of nutrients. Rotate between recipes to get a wide variety of ingredients and health benefits.

The Mediterranean Diet Four-Week Plan

The Mediterranean Diet Four-Week Plan serves as a pivotal foundation for anyone looking to embrace a healthier, more balanced lifestyle. This plan provides a structured approach to integrating the renowned heart-healthy and longevity-promoting principles of the Mediterranean diet into daily life. By offering a clear roadmap over a month, it ensures gradual adaptation, helping individuals internalize the habits, flavors, and rhythms of this diet. The four-week duration is crucial—it's believed that it takes about 21 days to form a new habit, and this plan extends beyond that threshold, solidifying dietary changes into sustainable practices. Moreover, by offering diverse meals and ingredients throughout the month, it ensures adequate nutritional intake and showcases the rich tapestry of Mediterranean cuisine. In essence, the Mediterranean Diet Four-Week Plan isn't just a meal guide; it's a transformative journey towards optimal health and well-being.

Some useful Mediterranean Diet advice

Start with Olive Oil: Replace butter, margarine, and other cooking fats with extra virgin olive oil, which is heart-healthy and versatile. Whether you're sautéing vegetables or making a salad dressing, olive oil should be your go-to.

Embrace Seafood: Aim to eat fish and seafood at least twice a week. Fatty fish like salmon, mackerel, and sardines are especially rich in omega-3 fatty acids, which promote heart health.

Whole Grains are Key: Swap out refined grains for whole ones. Instead of white bread or pasta, opt for whole wheat, barley, or ancient grains like quinoa and farro.

Limit Red Meat: Try to reduce your consumption of red meats, and when you do consume, choose lean cuts. Replace meat-centric meals with plant-based ones or use meat as a complementary ingredient rather than the main focus.

Diversify Your Protein: Beans, lentils, chickpeas, and other legumes are protein-rich and fiber-filled. They're a staple in Mediterranean cuisine, so try incorporating them into salads, soups, and stews.

4-Week Meal Plan

WEEK 1

Day	Breakfast	Lunch	Dinner
1	Kale-proscuitto Porridge 6	Slow Cooker Beef Stew 28	Braised Cauliflower With White Wine 39
2	Herby Artichoke Frittata With Ricotta 6	Spinach Chicken With Chickpeas 28	Feta & Zucchini Rosti Cakes 39
3	Cheesy Fig Pizzas With Garlic Oil 7	Chicken With Halloumi Cheese 29	Tasty Lentil Burgers 40
4	Tuna And Olive Salad Sandwiches 7	Dragon Pork Chops With Pickle Topping 29	Vegan Lentil Bolognese 40
5	Brown Rice Salad With Cheese 8	Beef & Pumpkin Stew 30	Cheesy Sweet Potato Burgers 41
6	Spinach And Egg Breakfast Wraps 8	Fennel Beef Ribs 30	Baked Vegetable Stew 41
7	Apple & Pumpkin Muffins 9	Citrus Chicken Wings 30	Garlicky Zucchini Cubes With Mint 42

WEEK 2

Day	Breakfast	Lunch	Dinner
1	Eggplant, Spinach, And Feta Sandwiches 9	Nutty Chicken Breasts 31	Balsamic Cherry Tomatoes 42
2	Nut & Plum Parfait 9	Tomato Caper & Turkey Pot 31	Paprika Cauliflower Steaks With Walnut Sauce 43
3	Morning Overnight Oats With Raspberries 10	Easy Pork Stew 32	Zoodles With Walnut Pesto 43
4	Bell Pepper & Cheese Egg Scramble 10	Bell Pepper & Olive Turkey Breasts 32	Beet And Watercress Salad 44
5	Vegetable & Hummus Bowl 10	Baked Peppery Parsnip & Pork 32	Mushroom Filled Zucchini Boats 44
6	Salmon Salad Wraps 11	Grilled Pork Chops With Apricot Chutney 33	Baked Honey Acorn Squash 45
7	Baked Eggs In Avocado 11	Tomato & Basil Chicken Breasts 33	Rainbow Vegetable Kebabs 45

WEEK 3

Day	Breakfast	Lunch	Dinner
1	Lazy Blueberry Oatmeal 11	Grilled Lemon Chicken 34	Wilted Dandelion Greens With Sweet Onion 45
2	Ricotta Muffins With Pear Glaze 12	Lamb Tagine With Couscous And Almonds 35	Roasted Vegetables And Chickpeas 46
3	Cream Peach Smoothie 12	Simple Chicken With Olive Tapenade 35	Simple Braised Carrots 46
4	Tomato Eggs With Fried Potatoes 12	Parsley Eggplant Lamb 36	Baked Veggie Medley 47
5	Hot Zucchini & Egg Nests 13	Eggplant & Turkey Moussaka 36	Mini Crustless Spinach Quiches 47
6	Pumpkin Pie Parfait 13	Chicken Thighs Al Orange 37	Baby Kale And Cabbage Salad 48
7	Skillet Eggplant & Kale Frittata 13	Tasty Chicken Pot 37	Fish & Chickpea Stew 48

WEEK 4

Day	Breakfast	Lunch	Dinner
1	Ham, Bean & Sweet Potato Frittata 14	Stewed Chicken Sausage With Farro 37	Buttery Garlic Green Beans 49
2	Classic Shakshuka 14	Deluxe Chicken With Yogurt Sauce 38	Creamy Polenta With Mushrooms 49
3	Green Veggie Sandwiches 15	Pork Millet With Chestnuts 38	Roasted Veggies And Brown Rice Bowl 50
4	Pecorino Bulgur & Spinach Cupcakes 15	Lemony Lamb Stew 55	Parsley & Olive Zucchini Bake 50
5	Cheesy Kale & Egg Cupcakes 16	Three-bean Salad With Black Olives 56	Stuffed Portobello Mushrooms With Spinach 51
6	Asparagus & Chicken Skillet 31	Cucumber Gazpacho 58	Spinach & Bean Salad With Goat Cheese 52
7	Drunken Lamb Bake 34	Pork Chop & Arugula Salad 59	Roasted Pepper & Tomato Soup 52

Measurement Conversions

BASIC KITCHEN CONVERSIONS & EQUIVALENTS

DRY MEASUREMENTS CONVERSION CHART

3 TEASPOONS = 1 TABLESPOON = 1/16 CUP

6 TEASPOONS = 2 TABLESPOONS = 1/8 CUP

12 TEASPOONS = 4 TABLESPOONS = 1/4 CUP

24 TEASPOONS = 8 TABLESPOONS = 1/2 CUP

36 TEASPOONS = 12 TABLESPOONS = 3/4 CUP

48 TEASPOONS = 16 TABLESPOONS = 1 CUP

METRIC TO US COOKING CONVERSIONS

OVEN TEMPERATURES

120 °C = 250 °F

160 °C = 320 °F

180° C = 350 °F

205 °C = 400 °F

220 °C = 425 °F

LIQUID MEASUREMENTS CONVERSION CHART

8 FLUID OUNCES = 1 CUP = 1/2 PINT = 1/4 QUART

16 FLUID OUNCES = 2 CUPS = 1 PINT = 1/2 QUART

32 FLUID OUNCES = 4 CUPS = 2 PINTS = 1 QUART
 = 1/4 GALLON

128 FLUID OUNCES = 16 CUPS = 8 PINTS = 4 QUARTS = 1 GALLON

BAKING IN GRAMS

1 CUP FLOUR = 140 GRAMS

1 CUP SUGAR = 150 GRAMS

1 CUP POWDERED SUGAR = 160 GRAMS

1 CUP HEAVY CREAM = 235 GRAMS

VOLUME

1 MILLILITER = 1/5 TEASPOON

5 ML = 1 TEASPOON

15 ML = 1 TABLESPOON

240 ML = 1 CUP OR 8 FLUID OUNCES

1 LITER = 34 FL. OUNCES

WEIGHT

1 GRAM = .035 OUNCES

100 GRAMS = 3.5 OUNCES

500 GRAMS = 1.1 POUNDS

1 KILOGRAM = 35 OUNCES

US TO METRIC COOKING CONVERSIONS

1/5 TSP = 1 ML

1 TSP = 5 ML

1 TBSP = 15 ML

1 FL OUNCE = 30 ML

1 CUP = 237 ML

1 PINT (2 CUPS) = 473 ML

1 QUART (4 CUPS) = .95 LITER

1 GALLON (16 CUPS) = 3.8 LITERS

1 OZ = 28 GRAMS

1 POUND = 454 GRAMS

BUTTER

1 CUP BUTTER = 2 STICKS = 8 OUNCES = 230 GRAMS = 8 TABLESPOONS

WHAT DOES 1 CUP EQUAL

1 CUP = 8 FLUID OUNCES

1 CUP = 16 TABLESPOONS

1 CUP = 48 TEASPOONS

1 CUP = 1/2 PINT

1 CUP = 1/4 QUART

1 CUP = 1/16 GALLON

1 CUP = 240 ML

BAKING PAN CONVERSIONS

1 CUP ALL-PURPOSE FLOUR = 4.5 OZ

1 CUP ROLLED OATS = 3 OZ 1 LARGE EGG = 1.7 OZ

1 CUP BUTTER = 8 OZ 1 CUP MILK = 8 OZ

1 CUP HEAVY CREAM = 8.4 OZ

1 CUP GRANULATED SUGAR = 7.1 OZ

1 CUP PACKED BROWN SUGAR = 7.75 OZ

1 CUP VEGETABLE OIL = 7.7 OZ

1 CUP UNSIFTED POWDERED SUGAR = 4.4 OZ

BAKING PAN CONVERSIONS

9-INCH ROUND CAKE PAN = 12 CUPS

10-INCH TUBE PAN = 16 CUPS

11-INCH BUNDT PAN = 12 CUPS

9-INCH SPRINGFORM PAN = 10 CUPS

9 X 5 INCH LOAF PAN = 8 CUPS

9-INCH SQUARE PAN = 8 CUPS

Breakfast Recipes

Kale-proscuitto Porridge

Servings:2
Cooking Time:30 Minutes
Ingredients:

- 1 tbsp olive oil
- 1 green onion, chopped
- 1 oz prosciutto, chopped
- 2 cups kale
- ¾ cup old-fashioned oats
- 2 tbsp Parmesan, grated
- Salt and black pepper to taste

Directions:

1. Warm the olive oil in a pan over medium heat. Sauté the onion and prosciutto and sauté for 4 minutes or until the prosciutto is crisp and the onion turns golden. Add the kale and stir for 5 minutes until wilted. Transfer to a bowl.
2. Add the oats to the pan and let them toast for 2 minutes. Add 1 ½ of water or chicken stock and bring to a boil. Reduce the heat to low, cover, and let the oats simmer for 10 minutes or until the liquid is absorbed and the oats are tender.
3. Stir in Parmesan cheese, and add the onions, prosciutto, and kale back to the pan and cook until creamy but not dry. Adjust the seasoning with salt and pepper and serve.

Nutrition Info:

- Info Per Serving: Calories: 258;Fat: 12g;Protein: 11g;Carbs: 29g.

Herby Artichoke Frittata With Ricotta

Servings:2
Cooking Time:20 Minutes
Ingredients:

- 4 oz canned artichoke hearts, quartered
- 2 tbsp olive oil
- 4 large eggs
- 1 tsp dried herbs
- Salt and black pepper to taste
- 1 cup kale, chopped
- 8 cherry tomatoes, halved
- ½ cup crumbled ricotta cheese

Directions:

1. Preheat oven to 360 F. In a bowl, whisk the eggs, herbs, salt, and pepper and whisk well with a fork. Set aside. Warm the olive oil in a skillet over medium heat. Sauté the kale, artichoke, and cherry tomatoes until just wilted, 1-2 minutes.
2. Pour the egg mixture over and let it cook for 3-4 minutes until the eggs begin to set on the bottom. Sprinkle with ricotta cheese on top. Place the skillet under the preheated broiler for 5 minutes until the frittata is firm in the center and golden brown on top. Invert the frittata onto a plate and slice in half. Serve warm.

Nutrition Info:

- Info Per Serving: Calories: 527;Fat: 47g;Protein: 21g;Carbs: 10g.

Cheesy Fig Pizzas With Garlic Oil

Servings:2
Cooking Time: 10 Minutes

Ingredients:

- Dough:
- 1 cup almond flour
- 1½ cups whole-wheat flour
- ¾ teaspoon instant or rapid-rise yeast
- 2 teaspoons raw honey
- 1¼ cups ice water
- 2 tablespoons extra-virgin olive oil
- 1¾ teaspoons sea salt
- Garlic Oil:
- 4 tablespoons extra-virgin olive oil, divided
- ½ teaspoon dried thyme
- 2 garlic cloves, minced
- ⅛ teaspoon sea salt
- ½ teaspoon freshly ground pepper
- Topping:
- 1 cup fresh basil leaves
- 1 cup crumbled feta cheese
- 8 ounces fresh figs, stemmed and quartered lengthwise
- 2 tablespoons raw honey

Directions:

1. Make the Dough:
2. Combine the flours, yeast, and honey in a food processor, pulse to combine well. Gently add water while pulsing. Let the dough sit for 10 minutes.
3. Mix the olive oil and salt in the dough and knead the dough until smooth. Wrap in plastic and refrigerate for at least 1 day.
4. Make the Garlic Oil:
5. Heat 2 tablespoons of olive oil in a nonstick skillet over medium-low heat until shimmering.
6. Add the thyme, garlic, salt, and pepper and sauté for 30 seconds or until fragrant. Set them aside until ready to use.
7. Make the pizzas:
8. Preheat the oven to 500ºF. Grease two baking sheets with 2 tablespoons of olive oil.
9. Divide the dough in half and shape into two balls. Press the balls into 13-inch rounds. Sprinkle the rounds with a tough of flour if they are sticky.
10. Top the rounds with the garlic oil and basil leaves, then arrange the rounds on the baking sheets. Scatter with feta cheese and figs.
11. Put the sheets in the preheated oven and bake for 9 minutes or until lightly browned. Rotate the pizza halfway through.
12. Remove the pizzas from the oven, then discard the bay leaves. Drizzle with honey. Let sit for 5 minutes and serve immediately.

Nutrition Info:

- Info Per Serving: Calories: 1350;Fat: 46.5g;Protein: 27.5g;Carbs: 221.9g.

Tuna And Olive Salad Sandwiches

Servings:4
Cooking Time: 0 Minutes

Ingredients:

- 3 tablespoons freshly squeezed lemon juice
- 2 tablespoons extra-virgin olive oil
- 1 garlic clove, minced
- ½ teaspoon freshly ground black pepper
- 2 cans tuna, drained
- 1 can sliced olives, any green or black variety
- ½ cup chopped fresh fennel, including fronds
- 8 slices whole-grain crusty bread

Directions:

1. In a medium bowl, whisk together the lemon juice, oil, garlic, and pepper. Add the tuna, olives and fennel to the bowl. Using a fork, separate the tuna into chunks and stir to incorporate all the ingredients.
2. Divide the tuna salad equally among 4 slices of bread. Top each with the remaining bread slices.
3. Let the sandwiches sit for at least 5 minutes so the zesty filling can soak into the bread before serving.

Nutrition Info:

- Info Per Serving: Calories: 952;Fat: 17.0g;Protein: 165.0g;Carbs: 37.0g.

Brown Rice Salad With Cheese

Servings:4
Cooking Time:10 Minutes
Ingredients:
- 2 tbsp olive oil
- ½ cup brown rice
- 1 lb watercress
- 1 Roma tomato, sliced
- 4 oz feta cheese, crumbled
- 2 tbsp fresh basil, chopped
- Salt and black pepper to taste
- 2 tbsp lemon juice
- ¼ tsp lemon zest

Directions:
1. Bring to a boil salted water in a pot over medium heat. Add in the rice and cook for 15-18 minutes. Drain and let cool completely. Whisk the olive oil, lemon zest, lemon juice, salt, and pepper in a salad bowl. Add in the watercress, cooled rice, and basil and toss to coat. Top with feta cheese and tomato. Serve immediately.

Nutrition Info:
- Info Per Serving: Calories: 480;Fat: 24g;Protein: 14g;Carbs: 55g.

Spinach And Egg Breakfast Wraps

Servings:2
Cooking Time: 7 Minutes
Ingredients:
- 1 tablespoon olive oil
- ¼ cup minced onion
- 3 to 4 tablespoons minced sun-dried tomatoes in olive oil and herbs
- 3 large eggs, whisked
- 1½ cups packed baby spinach
- 1 ounce crumbled feta cheese
- Salt, to taste
- 2 whole-wheat tortillas

Directions:
1. Heat the olive oil in a large skillet over medium-high heat.
2. Sauté the onion and tomatoes for about 3 minutes, stirring occasionally, until softened.
3. Reduce the heat to medium. Add the whisked eggs and stir-fry for 1 to 2 minutes.
4. Stir in the baby spinach and scatter with the crumbled feta cheese. Season as needed with salt.
5. Remove the egg mixture from the heat to a plate. Set aside.
6. Working in batches, place 2 tortillas on a microwave-safe dish and microwave for about 20 seconds to make them warm.
7. Spoon half of the egg mixture into each tortilla. Fold them in half and roll up, then serve.

Nutrition Info:
- Info Per Serving: Calories: 434;Fat: 28.1g;Protein: 17.2g;Carbs: 30.8g.

Apple & Pumpkin Muffins

Servings:12
Cooking Time:30 Minutes
Ingredients:

- ½ cup butter, melted
- 1 ½ cups granulated sugar
- ½ cup sugar
- ¾ cup flour
- 2 tsp pumpkin pie spice
- 1 tsp baking soda
- ¼ tsp salt
- ¼ tsp nutmeg
- 1 apple, grated
- 1 can pumpkin puree
- ½ cup full-fat yogurt
- 2 large egg whites

Directions:

1. Preheat the oven to 350 F. In a bowl, mix sugars, flour, pumpkin pie spice, baking soda, salt, and nutmeg. In a separate bowl, mix apple, pumpkin puree, yogurt, and butter.
2. Slowly mix the wet ingredients into the dry ingredients. Using a mixer on high, whip the egg whites until stiff and fold them into the batter. Pour the batter into a greased muffin tin, filling each cup halfway. Bake for 25 minutes or until a fork inserted in the center comes out clean. Let cool.

Nutrition Info:

- Info Per Serving: Calories: 259;Fat: 8.2g;Protein: 3g;Carbs: 49.1g.

Eggplant, Spinach, And Feta Sandwiches

Servings:2
Cooking Time: 6 To 8 Minutes
Ingredients:

- 1 medium eggplant, sliced into ½-inch-thick slices
- 2 tablespoons olive oil
- Sea salt and freshly ground pepper, to taste
- 5 to 6 tablespoons hummus
- 4 slices whole-wheat bread, toasted
- 1 cup baby spinach leaves
- 2 ounces feta cheese, softened

Directions:

1. Preheat the grill to medium-high heat.
2. Salt both sides of the sliced eggplant, and let sit for 20 minutes to draw out the bitter juices.
3. Rinse the eggplant and pat dry with a paper towel.
4. Brush the eggplant slices with olive oil and season with sea salt and freshly ground pepper to taste.
5. Grill the eggplant until lightly charred on both sides but still slightly firm in the middle, about 3 to 4 minutes per side.
6. Spread the hummus on the bread slices and top with the spinach leaves, feta cheese, and grilled eggplant. Top with the other slice of bread and serve immediately.

Nutrition Info:

- Info Per Serving: Calories: 493;Fat: 25.3g;Protein: 17.1g;Carbs: 50.9g.

Nut & Plum Parfait

Servings:4
Cooking Time:10 Minutes
Ingredients:

- 1 tbsp honey
- 1 cup plums, chopped
- 2 cups Greek yogurt
- 1 tsp cinnamon powder
- 1 tbsp almonds, chopped
- 1 tbsp walnuts, chopped
- ¼ cup pistachios, chopped

Directions:

1. Place a skillet over medium heat and add in plums, honey, cinnamon powder, almonds, walnuts, pistachios, and ¼ cup water. Cook for 5 minutes. Share Greek yogurt into serving bowls and top with plum mixture and toss before serving.

Nutrition Info:

- Info Per Serving: Calories: 200;Fat: 5g;Protein: 4g;Carbs: 42g.

Morning Overnight Oats With Raspberries

Servings:2
Cooking Time: 0 Minutes
Ingredients:

- ⅔ cup unsweetened almond milk
- ¼ cup raspberries
- ⅓ cup rolled oats
- 1 teaspoon honey
- ¼ teaspoon turmeric
- ⅛ teaspoon ground cinnamon
- Pinch ground cloves

Directions:

1. Place the almond milk, raspberries, rolled oats, honey, turmeric, cinnamon, and cloves in a mason jar. Cover and shake to combine.
2. Transfer to the refrigerator for at least 8 hours, preferably 24 hours.
3. Serve chilled.

Nutrition Info:

- Info Per Serving: Calories: 81;Fat: 1.9g;Protein: 2.1g;Carbs: 13.8g.

Bell Pepper & Cheese Egg Scramble

Servings:4
Cooking Time:20 Minutes
Ingredients:

- ½ cup fresh mozzarella cheese, crumbled
- 2 tsp olive oil
- 1 cup bell peppers, chopped
- 2 garlic cloves, minced
- 6 large eggs, beaten
- Salt to taste
- 2 tbsp fresh cilantro, chopped

Directions:

1. Warm the olive oil in a large skillet over medium heat. Add the peppers and sauté for 5 minutes, stirring occasionally. Add the garlic and cook for 1 minute. Stir in the eggs and salt and cook for 2-3 minutes until the eggs begin to set on the bottom. Top with mozzarella cheese and cook the eggs for about 2 more minutes, stirring slowly, until the eggs are soft-set and custardy. Sprinkle with cilantro and serve.

Nutrition Info:

- Info Per Serving: Calories: 259;Fat: 16g;Protein: 29g;Carbs: 2g.

Vegetable & Hummus Bowl

Servings:4
Cooking Time:15 Minutes
Ingredients:

- 2 tbsp butter
- 2 tbsp olive oil
- 3 cups green cabbage, shredded
- 3 cups kale, chopped
- 1 lb asparagus, chopped
- ½ cup hummus
- 1 avocado, sliced
- 4 boiled eggs, sliced
- 1 tbsp balsamic vinegar
- 1 garlic clove, minced
- 2 tsp yellow mustard
- Salt and black pepper to taste

Directions:

1. Melt butter in a skillet over medium heat and sauté asparagus for 5 minutes. Mix the olive oil, balsamic vinegar, garlic, yellow mustard, salt, and pepper in a bowl. Spoon the hummus onto the center of a salad bowl and arrange in the asparagus, kale, cabbage, and avocado. Top with the egg slices. Drizzle with the dressing and serve.

Nutrition Info:

- Info Per Serving: Calories: 392;Fat: 31g;Protein: 14g;Carbs: 22g.

Salmon Salad Wraps

Servings:6
Cooking Time: 0 Minutes
Ingredients:

- 1 pound salmon fillets, cooked and flaked
- ½ cup diced carrots
- ½ cup diced celery
- 3 tablespoons diced red onion
- 3 tablespoons chopped fresh dill
- 2 tablespoons capers
- 1½ tablespoons extra-virgin olive oil
- 1 tablespoon aged balsamic vinegar
- ¼ teaspoon kosher or sea salt
- ½ teaspoon freshly ground black pepper
- 4 whole-wheat flatbread wraps or soft whole-wheat tortillas

Directions:
1. In a large bowl, stir together all the ingredients, except for the wraps.
2. On a clean work surface, lay the wraps. Divide the salmon mixture evenly among the wraps. Fold up the bottom of the wraps, then roll up the wrap.
3. Serve immediately.

Nutrition Info:
- Info Per Serving: Calories: 194;Fat: 8.0g;Protein: 18.0g;Carbs: 13.0g.

Baked Eggs In Avocado

Servings:2
Cooking Time: 10 To 15 Minutes
Ingredients:

- 1 ripe large avocado
- 2 large eggs
- Salt and freshly ground black pepper, to taste
- 4 tablespoons jarred pesto, for serving
- 2 tablespoons chopped tomato, for serving
- 2 tablespoons crumbled feta cheese, for serving (optional)

Directions:
1. Preheat the oven to 425°F.
2. Slice the avocado in half, remove the pit and scoop out a generous tablespoon of flesh from each half to create a hole big enough to fit an egg.
3. Transfer the avocado halves (cut-side up) to a baking sheet.
4. Crack 1 egg into each avocado half and sprinkle with salt and pepper.
5. Bake in the preheated oven for 10 to 15 minutes, or until the eggs are cooked to your preferred doneness.
6. Remove the avocado halves from the oven. Scatter each avocado half evenly with the jarred pesto, chopped tomato, and crumbled feta cheese (if desired). Serve immediately.

Nutrition Info:
- Info Per Serving: Calories: 301;Fat: 25.9g;Protein: 8.1g;Carbs: 9.8g.

Lazy Blueberry Oatmeal

Servings:2
Cooking Time:10 Min + Chilling Time
Ingredients:

- ⅔ cup milk
- ⅓ cup quick rolled oats
- ¼ cup blueberries
- 1 tsp honey
- ½ tsp ground cinnamon
- ¼ tsp ground cloves

Directions:
1. Layer the oats, milk, blueberries, honey, cinnamon, and cloves into 2 mason jars. Cover and store in the refrigerator overnight. Serve cold and enjoy!

Nutrition Info:
- Info Per Serving: Calories: 82;Fat: 2.2g;Protein: 2g;Carbs: 14.1g.

Ricotta Muffins With Pear Glaze

Servings:4
Cooking Time:42 Minutes
Ingredients:

- 16 oz ricotta cheese
- 2 large eggs
- ¼ cup flour
- 1 tbsp sugar
- 1 tsp vanilla extract
- ¼ tsp ground nutmeg
- 1 pear, cored and diced
- 1 tbsp sugar

Directions:

1. Preheat the oven to 400 F. In a large bowl, whisk the ricotta, eggs, flour, sugar, vanilla, and nutmeg. Spoon into 4 greased ramekins. Bake for 20-25 minutes. Transfer to a wire rack to cool before unmolding.
2. Place the pear, sugar, and 2 tbsp of water in a small saucepan over low heat. Simmer for 10 minutes until slightly softened. Remove from the heat, and stir in the honey. Serve the ricotta ramekins glazed with pear sauce.

Nutrition Info:

- Info Per Serving: Calories: 329;Fat: 19g;Protein: 17g;Carbs: 23g.

Cream Peach Smoothie

Servings:1
Cooking Time:5 Minutes
Ingredients:

- 1 large peach, sliced
- 6 oz peach Greek yogurt
- 2 tbsp almond milk
- 2 ice cubes

Directions:

1. Blend the peach, yogurt, almond milk, and ice cubes in your food processor until thick and creamy. Serve and enjoy!

Nutrition Info:

- Info Per Serving: Calories: 228;Fat: 3g;Protein: 11g;Carbs: 41.6g.

Tomato Eggs With Fried Potatoes

Servings:2
Cooking Time:20 Minutes
Ingredients:

- 2 tbsp + ½ cup olive oil
- 3 medium tomatoes, puréed
- 1 tbsp fresh tarragon, chopped
- 1 garlic clove, minced
- Salt and black pepper to taste
- 3 potatoes, cubed
- 4 fresh eggs
- 1 tsp fresh oregano, chopped

Directions:

1. Warm 2 tbsp of olive oil in a saucepan over medium heat. Add the garlic and sauté for 1 minute. Pour in the tomatoes, tarragon, salt, and pepper. Reduce the heat and cook for 5-8 minutes or until the sauce is thickened and bubbly.
2. Warm the remaining olive oil in a skillet over medium heat. Fry the potatoes for 5 minutes until crisp and browned on the outside, then cover and reduce heat to low. Steam potatoes until done. Carefully crack the eggs into the tomato sauce.
3. Cook over low heat until the eggs are set in the sauce, about 6 minutes. Remove the potatoes from the pan, drain them on paper towels, and place them in a bowl. Sprinkle with salt and pepper and top with oregano. Carefully remove the eggs with a slotted spoon and place them on a plate with the potatoes. Spoon sauce over and serve.

Nutrition Info:

- Info Per Serving: Calories: 1146;Fat: 69g;Protein: 26g;Carbs: 45g.

Hot Zucchini & Egg Nests

Servings:4
Cooking Time:25 Minutes
Ingredients:

- 2 tbsp olive oil
- 4 eggs
- 1 lb zucchinis, shredded
- Salt and black pepper to taste
- ½ red chili pepper, minced
- 2 tbsp parsley, chopped

Directions:

1. Preheat the oven to 360 F. Combine zucchini, salt, pepper, and olive oil in a bowl. Form nest shapes with a spoon onto a greased baking sheet. Crack an egg into each nest and season with salt, pepper, and chili pepper. Bake for 11 minutes. Serve topped with parsley.

Nutrition Info:

- Info Per Serving: Calories: 141;Fat: 11.6g;Protein: 7g;Carbs: 4.2g.

Pumpkin Pie Parfait

Servings:4
Cooking Time: 0 Minutes
Ingredients:

- 1 can pure pumpkin purée
- 4 teaspoons honey
- 1 teaspoon pumpkin pie spice
- ¼ teaspoon ground cinnamon
- 2 cups plain Greek yogurt
- 1 cup honey granola

Directions:

1. Combine the pumpkin purée, honey, pumpkin pie spice, and cinnamon in a large bowl and stir to mix well.
2. Cover the bowl with plastic wrap and chill in the refrigerator for at least 2 hours.
3. Make the parfaits: Layer each parfait glass with ¼ cup pumpkin mixture in the bottom. Top with ¼ cup of yogurt and scatter each top with ¼ cup of honey granola. Repeat the layers until the glasses are full.
4. Serve immediately.

Nutrition Info:

- Info Per Serving: Calories: 263;Fat: 8.9g;Protein: 15.3g;Carbs: 34.6g.

Skillet Eggplant & Kale Frittata

Servings:1
Cooking Time:20 Minutes
Ingredients:

- 1 tbsp olive oil
- 3 large eggs
- 1 tsp milk
- 1 cup curly kale, torn
- ½ eggplant, peeled and diced
- ¼ red bell pepper, chopped
- Salt and black pepper to taste
- 1 oz crumbled Goat cheese

Directions:

1. Preheat your broiler. Whisk the eggs with milk, salt, and pepper until just combined. Heat the olive oil in a small skillet over medium heat. Spread the eggs on the bottom and add the kale on top in an even layer; top with veggies.
2. Season with salt and pepper. Allow the eggs and vegetables to cook 3 to 5 minutes until the bottom half of the eggs are firm and vegetables are tender. Top with the crumbled Goat cheese and place under the broiler for 5 minutes until the eggs are firm in the middle and the cheese has melted. Slice into wedges and serve immediately.

Nutrition Info:

- Info Per Serving: Calories: 622;Fat: 39g;Protein: 41g;Carbs: 33g.

Ham, Bean & Sweet Potato Frittata

Servings:4
Cooking Time:25 Minutes
Ingredients:
- 2 sweet potatoes, boiled and chopped
- 2 tbsp olive oil
- 4 eggs, whisked
- 1 red onion, chopped
- ¾ cup ham, chopped
- ½ cup white beans, cooked
- 2 tbsp Greek yogurt
- Salt and black pepper to taste
- 10 cherry tomatoes, halved
- ¾ cup cheddar cheese, grated

Directions:

1. Warm the olive oil in a skillet over medium heat and sauté onion for 2 minutes. Stir in sweet potatoes, ham, beans, yogurt, salt, pepper, and tomatoes and cook for another 3 minutes. Pour in eggs and cheese, lock the lid and cook for an additional 10 minutes. Cut before serving.

Nutrition Info:
- Info Per Serving: Calories: 280;Fat: 18g;Protein: 12g;Carbs: 9g.

Classic Shakshuka

Servings:2
Cooking Time: 30 Minutes
Ingredients:
- 1 tablespoon olive oil
- ½ red pepper, diced
- ½ medium onion, diced
- 2 small garlic cloves, minced
- ½ teaspoon smoked paprika
- ½ teaspoon cumin
- Pinch red pepper flakes
- 1 can fire-roasted tomatoes
- ¼ teaspoon salt
- Pinch freshly ground black pepper
- 1 ounce crumbled feta cheese (about ¼ cup)
- 3 large eggs
- 3 tablespoons minced fresh parsley

Directions:

1. Heat the olive oil in a skillet over medium-high heat and add the pepper, onion, and garlic. Sauté until the vegetables start to turn golden.
2. Add the paprika, cumin, and red pepper flakes and stir to toast the spices for about 30 seconds. Add the tomatoes with their juices.
3. Reduce the heat and let the sauce simmer for 10 minutes, or until it starts to thicken. Add the salt and pepper. Taste the sauce and adjust seasonings as necessary.
4. Scatter the feta cheese on top. Make 3 wells in the sauce and crack one egg into each well.
5. Cover and let the eggs cook for about 7 minutes. Remove the lid and continue cooking for 5 minutes more, or until the yolks are cooked to desired doneness.
6. Garnish with fresh parsley and serve.

Nutrition Info:
- Info Per Serving: Calories: 289;Fat: 18.2g;Protein: 15.1g;Carbs: 18.5g.

Green Veggie Sandwiches

Servings:2
Cooking Time: 0 Minutes
Ingredients:

- Spread:
- 1 can cannellini beans, drained and rinsed
- ⅓ cup packed fresh basil leaves
- ⅓ cup packed fresh parsley
- ⅓ cup chopped fresh chives
- 2 garlic cloves, chopped
- Zest and juice of ½ lemon
- 1 tablespoon apple cider vinegar

- Sandwiches:
- 4 whole-grain bread slices, toasted
- 8 English cucumber slices
- 1 large beefsteak tomato, cut into slices
- 1 large avocado, halved, pitted, and cut into slices
- 1 small yellow bell pepper, cut into slices
- 2 handfuls broccoli sprouts
- 2 handfuls fresh spinach

Directions:

1. Make the Spread
2. In a food processor, combine the cannellini beans, basil, parsley, chives, garlic, lemon zest and juice, and vinegar. Pulse a few times, scrape down the sides, and purée until smooth. You may need to scrape down the sides again to incorporate all the basil and parsley. Refrigerate for at least 1 hour to allow the flavors to blend.
3. Assemble the Sandwiches
4. Build your sandwiches by spreading several tablespoons of spread on each slice of bread. Layer two slices of bread with the cucumber, tomato, avocado, bell pepper, broccoli sprouts, and spinach. Top with the remaining bread slices and press down lightly.
5. Serve immediately.

Nutrition Info:

- Info Per Serving: Calories: 617;Fat: 21.1g;Protein: 28.1g;Carbs: 86.1g.

Pecorino Bulgur & Spinach Cupcakes

Servings:6
Cooking Time:45 Minutes
Ingredients:

- 2 eggs, whisked
- 1 cup bulgur
- 3 cups water
- 1 cup spinach, torn
- 2 spring onions, chopped
- ¼ cup Pecorino cheese, grated
- ½ tsp garlic powder
- Sea salt and pepper to taste
- ½ tsp dried oregano

Directions:

1. Preheat the oven to 340 F. Grease a muffin tin with cooking spray. Warm 2 cups of salted water in a saucepan over medium heat and add in bulgur. Bring to a boil and cook for 10-15 minutes. Remove to a bowl and fluff with a fork. Stir in spinach, spring onions, eggs, Pecorino cheese, garlic powder, salt, pepper, and oregano. Divide between muffin holes and bake for 25 minutes. Serve chilled.

Nutrition Info:

- Info Per Serving: Calories: 280;Fat: 12g;Protein: 5g;Carbs: 9g.

Cheesy Kale & Egg Cupcakes

Servings:2
Cooking Time:30 Minutes

Ingredients:

- ¼ cup kale, chopped
- 3 eggs
- 1 leek, sliced
- 4 tbsp Parmesan, grated
- 2 tbsp almond milk
- 1 red bell pepper, chopped
- Salt and black pepper to taste
- 1 tomato, chopped
- 2 tbsp mozzarella, grated

Directions:

1. Preheat the oven to 360 F. Grease a muffin tin with cooking spray. Whisk the eggs in a bowl. Add in milk, kale, leek, Parmesan cheese, bell pepper, salt, black pepper, tomato, and mozzarella cheese and stir to combine. Divide the mixture between the cases and bake for 20-25 minutes. Let cool completely on a wire rack before serving.

Nutrition Info:

- Info Per Serving: Calories: 320;Fat: 20g;Protein: 26g;Carbs: 9g.

Fish And Seafood Recipes

Prawns With Mushrooms

Servings:4
Cooking Time:25 Minutes
Ingredients:

- 1 lb tiger prawns, peeled and deveined
- 3 tbsp olive oil
- 2 green onions, sliced
- ½ lb white mushrooms, sliced
- 2 tbsp balsamic vinegar
- 2 tsp garlic, minced

Directions:
1. Warm the olive oil in a skillet over medium heat and cook green onions and garlic for 2 minutes. Stir in mushrooms and balsamic vinegar and cook for an additional 6 minutes. Put in prawns and cook for 4 minutes. Serve right away.

Nutrition Info:
- Info Per Serving: Calories: 260;Fat: 9g;Protein: 19g;Carbs: 13g.

Lemon-garlic Sea Bass

Servings:2
Cooking Time:25 Minutes
Ingredients:

- 2 tbsp olive oil
- 2 sea bass fillets
- 1 lemon, juiced
- 4 garlic cloves, minced
- Salt and black pepper to taste

Directions:
1. Preheat the oven to 380F. Line a baking sheet with parchment paper. Brush sea bass fillets with lemon juice, olive oil, garlic, salt, and pepper and arrange them on the sheet. Bake for 15 minutes. Serve with salad.

Nutrition Info:
- Info Per Serving: Calories: 530;Fat: 30g;Protein: 54g;Carbs: 15g.

Garlic-butter Parmesan Salmon And Asparagus

Servings:2
Cooking Time: 15 Minutes
Ingredients:

- 2 salmon fillets, skin on and patted dry
- Pink Himalayan salt
- Freshly ground black pepper, to taste
- 1 pound fresh asparagus, ends snapped off
- 3 tablespoons almond butter
- 2 garlic cloves, minced
- ¼ cup grated Parmesan cheese

Directions:
1. Preheat the oven to 400°F. Line a baking sheet with aluminum foil.
2. Season both sides of the salmon fillets with salt and pepper.
3. Put the salmon in the middle of the baking sheet and arrange the asparagus around the salmon.
4. Heat the almond butter in a small saucepan over medium heat.
5. Add the minced garlic and cook for about 3 minutes, or until the garlic just begins to brown.
6. Drizzle the garlic-butter sauce over the salmon and asparagus and scatter the Parmesan cheese on top.
7. Bake in the preheated oven for about 12 minutes, or until the salmon is cooked through and the asparagus is crisp-tender. You can switch the oven to broil at the end of cooking time for about 3 minutes to get a nice char on the asparagus.
8. Let cool for 5 minutes before serving.

Nutrition Info:
- Info Per Serving: Calories: 435;Fat: 26.1g;Protein: 42.3g;Carbs: 10.0g.

Seared Salmon With Lemon Cream Sauce

Servings:4

Cooking Time: 20 Minutes

Ingredients:

- 4 salmon fillets
- Sea salt and freshly ground black pepper, to taste
- 1 tablespoon extra-virgin olive oil
- ½ cup low-sodium vegetable broth
- Juice and zest of 1 lemon
- 1 teaspoon chopped fresh thyme
- ½ cup fat-free sour cream
- 1 teaspoon honey
- 1 tablespoon chopped fresh chives

Directions:

1. Preheat the oven to 400ºF.
2. Season the salmon lightly on both sides with salt and pepper.
3. Place a large ovenproof skillet over medium-high heat and add the olive oil.
4. Sear the salmon fillets on both sides until golden, about 3 minutes per side.
5. Transfer the salmon to a baking dish and bake in the preheated oven until just cooked through, about 10 minutes.
6. Meanwhile, whisk together the vegetable broth, lemon juice and zest, and thyme in a small saucepan over medium-high heat until the liquid reduces by about one-quarter, about 5 minutes.
7. Whisk in the sour cream and honey.
8. Stir in the chives and serve the sauce over the salmon.

Nutrition Info:

- Info Per Serving: Calories: 310;Fat: 18.0g;Protein: 29.0g;Carbs: 6.0g.

Roasted Red Snapper With Citrus Topping

Servings:2

Cooking Time:35 Minutes

Ingredients:

- 2 tbsp olive oil
- 1 tsp fresh cilantro, chopped
- ½ tsp grated lemon zest
- ½ tbsp lemon juice
- ½ tsp grated grapefruit zest
- ½ tbsp grapefruit juice
- ½ tsp grated orange zest
- ½ tbsp orange juice
- ½ shallot, minced
- ¼ tsp red pepper flakes
- Salt and black pepper to taste
- 1 whole red snapper, cleaned

Directions:

1. Preheat oven to 380F. Whisk the olive oil, cilantro, lemon juice, orange juice, grapefruit juice, shallot, and pepper flakes together in a bowl. Season with salt and pepper. Set aside the citrus topping until ready to serve.

2. In a separate bowl, combine lemon zest, orange zest, grapefruit zest, salt, and pepper. With a sharp knife, make 3-4 shallow slashes, about 2 inches apart, on both sides of the snapper. Spoon the citrus mixture into the fish cavity and transfer to a greased baking sheet. Roast for 25 minutes until the fish flakes. Serve drizzled with citrus topping, and enjoy!

Nutrition Info:

- Info Per Serving: Calories: 257;Fat: 21g;Protein: 16g;Carbs: 1.6g.

North African Grilled Fish Fillets

Servings:4

Cooking Time:15 Minutes

Ingredients:

- 1 tbsp olive oil
- 1 tsp harissa seasoning
- 4 fish fillets
- 2 lemons, sliced
- 2 tbsp lemon juice
- Salt and black pepper to taste

Directions:

1. Preheat your grill to 400 F. In a bowl, whisk the lemon juice, olive oil, harissa seasoning, salt, and pepper. Coat both sides of the fish with the mixture. Carefully place the lemon slices on the grill, arranging 3-4 slices together in the shape of a fish fillet, and repeat with the remaining slices. Place the fish fillets directly on top of the lemon slices and grill with the lid closed. Turn the fish halfway through the cooking time only if the fillets are more than half an inch thick. The fish is done and ready to serve when it just begins to separate into chunks when pressed gently with a fork. Serve and enjoy!

Nutrition Info:

- Info Per Serving: Calories: 208;Fat: 12g;Protein: 21g;Carbs: 2g.

Canned Sardine Donburi (rice Bowl)

Servings:4

Cooking Time: 40 To 50 Minutes

Ingredients:

- 4 cups water
- 2 cups brown rice, rinsed well
- ½ teaspoon salt
- 3 cans sardines packed in water, drained
- 3 scallions, sliced thin
- 1-inch piece fresh ginger, grated
- 4 tablespoons sesame oil

Directions:

1. Place the water, brown rice, and salt to a large saucepan and stir to combine. Allow the mixture to boil over high heat.
2. Once boiling, reduce the heat to low, and cook covered for 45 to 50 minutes, or until the rice is tender.
3. Meanwhile, roughly mash the sardines with a fork in a medium bowl.
4. When the rice is done, stir in the mashed sardines, scallions, and ginger.
5. Divide the mixture into four bowls. Top each bowl with a drizzle of sesame oil. Serve warm.

Nutrition Info:

- Info Per Serving: Calories: 603;Fat: 23.6g;Protein: 25.2g;Carbs: 73.8g.

Creamy Halibut & Potato Soup

Servings:4

Cooking Time:25 Minutes

Ingredients:

- 3 gold potatoes, peeled and cubed
- 4 oz halibut fillets, boneless and cubed
- 2 tbsp olive oil
- 2 carrots, chopped
- 1 red onion, chopped
- Salt and white pepper to taste
- 4 cups fish stock
- ½ cup heavy cream
- 1 tbsp dill, chopped

Directions:

1. Warm the olive oil in a skillet over medium heat and cook the onion for 3 minutes. Put in potatoes, salt, pepper, carrots, and stock and bring to a boil. Cook for an additional 5-6 minutes. Stir in halibut, cream, and dill and simmer for another 5 minutes. Serve right away.

Nutrition Info:

- Info Per Serving: Calories: 215;Fat: 17g;Protein: 12g;Carbs: 7g.

Parsley Littleneck Clams In Sherry Sauce

Servings:4
Cooking Time:20 Minutes
Ingredients:

- 2 tbsp olive oil
- 1 cup dry sherry
- 3 shallots, minced
- 4 garlic cloves, minced
- 4 lb littleneck clams, scrubbed
- 2 tbsp minced fresh parsley
- ½ tsp cayenne pepper
- 1 Lemon, cut into wedges

Directions:

1. Bring the sherry wine, shallots, and garlic to a simmer in a large saucepan and cook for 3 minutes. Add clams, cover, and cook, stirring twice, until clams open, about 7 minutes. With a slotted spoon, transfer clams to a serving bowl, discarding any that refuse to open. Stir in olive oil, parsley, and cayenne pepper. Pour sauce over clams and serve with lemon wedges.

Nutrition Info:

- Info Per Serving: Calories: 333;Fat: 9g;Protein: 44.9g;Carbs: 14g.

Tomato Seafood Soup

Servings:4
Cooking Time:30 Minutes
Ingredients:

- ½ lb cod, skinless and cubed
- 2 tbsp olive oil
- ½ lb shrimp, deveined
- 1 yellow onion, chopped
- 1 carrot, finely chopped
- 1 celery stalk, finely chopped
- 1 small pepper, chopped
- 1 garlic clove, minced
- ½ cup tomatoes, crushed
- 4 cups fish stock
- ¼ tsp rosemary, dried
- Salt and black pepper to taste

Directions:

1. Warm the olive oil in a pot over medium heat. Cook onion, garlic, carrot, celery, and pepper for 5 minutes until soft, stirring occasionally. Stir in the tomatoes, stock, cod, shrimp, rosemary, salt, and pepper and simmer for 15 minutes.

Nutrition Info:

- Info Per Serving: Calories: 200;Fat: 9g;Protein: 27g;Carbs: 5g.

Parsley Halibut With Roasted Peppers

Servings:4
Cooking Time:45 Minutes
Ingredients:

- 3 tbsp olive oil
- 1 tsp butter
- 2 red peppers, cut into wedges
- 4 halibut fillets
- 2 shallots, cut into rings
- 2 garlic cloves, minced
- ¾ cup breadcrumbs
- 2 tbsp chopped fresh parsley
- Salt and black pepper to taste

Directions:

1. Preheat oven to 450 F. Combine red peppers, garlic, shallots, 1 tbsp of olive oil, salt, and pepper in a bowl. Spread on a baking sheet and bake for 40 minutes. Warm the remaining olive oil in a pan over medium heat and brown the breadcrumbs for 4-5 minutes, stirring constantly. Set aside.

2. Clean the pan and add in the butter to melt. Sprinkle the fish with salt and pepper. Add to the butter and cook for 8-10 minutes on both sides. Divide the pepper mixture between 4 plates and top with halibut fillets. Spread the crunchy breadcrumbs all over and top with parsley. Serve and enjoy!

Nutrition Info:

- Info Per Serving: Calories: 511;Fat: 19.4g;Protein: 64g;Carbs: 18g.

Traditional Tuscan Scallops

Servings:4

Cooking Time:25 Minutes

Ingredients:

- 2 tbsp olive oil
- 1 lb sea scallops, rinsed
- 4 cups Tuscan kale
- 1 orange, juiced
- Salt and black pepper to taste
- ¼ tsp red pepper flakes

Directions:

1. Sprinkle scallops with salt and pepper.
2. Warm olive oil in a skillet over medium heat and brown scallops for 6-8 minutes on all sides. Remove to a plate and keep warm, covering with foil. In the same skillet, add the kale, red pepper flakes, orange juice, salt, and pepper and cook until the kale wilts, about 4-5 minutes. Share the kale mixture into 4 plates and top with the scallops. Serve warm.

Nutrition Info:

- Info Per Serving: Calories: 214;Fat: 8g;Protein: 21g;Carbs: 15.2g.

Tuna And Zucchini Patties

Servings:4

Cooking Time: 12 Minutes

Ingredients:

- 3 slices whole-wheat sandwich bread, toasted
- 2 cans tuna in olive oil, drained
- 1 cup shredded zucchini
- 1 large egg, lightly beaten
- ¼ cup diced red bell pepper
- 1 tablespoon dried oregano
- 1 teaspoon lemon zest
- ¼ teaspoon freshly ground black pepper
- ¼ teaspoon kosher or sea salt
- 1 tablespoon extra-virgin olive oil
- Salad greens or 4 whole-wheat rolls, for serving (optional)

Directions:

1. Crumble the toast into bread crumbs with your fingers (or use a knife to cut into ¼-inch cubes) until you have 1 cup of loosely packed crumbs. Pour the crumbs into a large bowl. Add the tuna, zucchini, beaten egg, bell pepper, oregano, lemon zest, black pepper, and salt. Mix well with a fork. With your hands, form the mixture into four (½-cup-size) patties. Place them on a plate, and press each patty flat to about ¾-inch thick.
2. In a large skillet over medium-high heat, heat the oil until it's very hot, about 2 minutes.
3. Add the patties to the hot oil, then reduce the heat down to medium. Cook the patties for 5 minutes, flip with a spatula, and cook for an additional 5 minutes. Serve the patties on salad greens or whole-wheat rolls, if desired.

Nutrition Info:

- Info Per Serving: Calories: 757;Fat: 72.0g;Protein: 5.0g;Carbs: 26.0g.

Roasted Salmon With Tomatoes & Capers

Servings:4

Cooking Time:25 Minutes

Ingredients:

- 1 tbsp olive oil
- 4 salmon steaks
- Salt and black pepper to taste
- ¼ mustard powder
- ½ tsp garlic powder
- 2 Roma tomatoes, chopped
- ¼ cup green olives, chopped
- 1 tsp capers
- ½ cup breadcrumbs
- 1 lemon, cut into wedges

Directions:

1. Preheat oven to 375 F. Arrange the salmon fillets on a greased baking dish. Season with salt, pepper, garlic powder, and mustard powder and coat with the breadcrumbs. Drizzle with olive oil. Scatter the tomatoes, green olives, garlic, and capers around the fish fillets. Bake for 15 minutes until the salmon steaks flake easily with a fork. Serve with lemon wedges.

Nutrition Info:

- Info Per Serving: Calories: 504;Fat: 18g;Protein: 68g;Carbs: 14g.

Pan-fried Chili Sea Scallops

Servings:4

Cooking Time:25 Minutes

Ingredients:

- 1 ½ lb large sea scallops, tendons removed
- 3 tbsp olive oil
- 1 garlic clove, finely chopped
- ½ red pepper flakes
- 2 tbsp chili sauce
- ¼ cup tomato sauce
- 1 small shallot, minced
- 1 tbsp minced fresh cilantro
- Salt and black pepper to taste

Directions:

1. Warm the olive oil in a skillet over medium heat. Add the scallops and cook for 2 minutes without moving them. Flip them and continue to cook for 2 more minutes, without moving them, until golden browned. Set aside. Add the shallot and garlic to the skillet and sauté for 3-5 minutes until softened. Pour in the chili sauce, tomato sauce, and red pepper flakes and stir for 3-4 minutes. Add the scallops back and warm through. Adjust the taste and top with cilantro.

Nutrition Info:

- Info Per Serving: Calories: 204;Fat: 14.1g;Protein: 14g;Carbs: 5g.

Braised Branzino With Wine Sauce

Servings:2
Cooking Time: 15 Minutes
Ingredients:

- Sauce:
- ¾ cup dry white wine
- 2 tablespoons white wine vinegar
- 2 tablespoons cornstarch
- 1 tablespoon honey
- Fish:
- 1 large branzino, butterflied and patted dry
- 2 tablespoons onion powder
- 2 tablespoons paprika
- ½ tablespoon salt
- 6 tablespoons extra-virgin olive oil, divided
- 4 garlic cloves, thinly sliced
- 4 scallions, both green and white parts, thinly sliced
- 1 large tomato, cut into ¼-inch cubes
- 4 kalamata olives, pitted and chopped

Directions:

1. Make the sauce: Mix together the white wine, vinegar, cornstarch, and honey in a bowl and keep stirring until the honey has dissolved. Set aside.
2. Make the fish: Place the fish on a clean work surface, skin-side down. Sprinkle the onion powder, paprika, and salt to season. Drizzle 2 tablespoons of olive oil all over the fish.
3. Heat 2 tablespoons of olive oil in a large skillet over high heat until it shimmers.
4. Add the fish, skin-side up, to the skillet and brown for about 2 minutes. Carefully flip the fish and cook for another 3 minutes. Remove from the heat to a plate and set aside.
5. Add the remaining 2 tablespoons olive oil to the skillet and swirl to coat. Stir in the garlic cloves, scallions, tomato, and kalamata olives and sauté for 5 minutes. Pour in the prepared sauce and stir to combine.
6. Return the fish (skin-side down) to the skillet, flipping to coat in the sauce. Reduce the heat to medium-low, and cook for an additional 5 minutes until cooked through.
7. Using a slotted spoon, transfer the fish to a plate and serve warm.

Nutrition Info:

- Info Per Serving: Calories: 1059;Fat: 71.9g;Protein: 46.2g;Carbs: 55.8g.

Baked Lemon Salmon

Servings:4
Cooking Time: 20 Minutes
Ingredients:

- ¼ teaspoon dried thyme
- Zest and juice of ½ lemon
- ¼ teaspoon salt
- ½ teaspoon freshly ground black pepper
- 1 pound salmon fillet
- Nonstick cooking spray

Directions:

1. Preheat the oven to 425ºF. Coat a baking sheet with nonstick cooking spray.
2. Mix together the thyme, lemon zest and juice, salt, and pepper in a small bowl and stir to incorporate.
3. Arrange the salmon, skin-side down, on the coated baking sheet. Spoon the thyme mixture over the salmon and spread it all over.
4. Bake in the preheated oven for about 15 to 20 minutes, or until the fish flakes apart easily. Serve warm.

Nutrition Info:

- Info Per Serving: Calories: 162;Fat: 7.0g;Protein: 23.1g;Carbs: 1.0g.

Shrimp & Gnocchi With Feta Cheese

Servings:4
Cooking Time:30 Minutes
Ingredients:

- 1 lb shrimp, shells and tails removed
- 1 jar roasted red peppers, chopped
- 2 tbsp olive oil
- 1 cup chopped fresh tomato
- 2 garlic cloves, minced
- ½ tsp dried oregano
- Black pepper to taste
- ¼ tsp crushed red peppers
- 1 lb potato gnocchi
- ½ cup cubed feta cheese
- ⅓ cup fresh basil leaves, torn

Directions:

1. Preheat oven to 425 F. In a baking dish, mix the tomatoes, olive oil, garlic, oregano, black pepper, and crushed red peppers. Roast in the oven for 10 minutes. Stir in the roasted peppers and shrimp. Roast for 10 minutes until the shrimp turn pink. Bring a saucepan of salted water to the boil and cook the gnocchi for 1-2 mins, until floating. Drain. Remove the dish from the oven. Mix in the cooked gnocchi, sprinkle with feta and basil and serve.

Nutrition Info:

- Info Per Serving: Calories: 146;Fat: 5g;Protein: 23g;Carbs: 1g.

Hot Tomato & Caper Squid Stew

Servings:4
Cooking Time:50 Minutes
Ingredients:

- 1 cans whole peeled tomatoes, diced
- ¼ cup olive oil
- 1 onion, chopped
- 1 celery rib, sliced
- 3 garlic cloves, minced
- ¼ tsp red pepper flakes
- 1 red chili, minced
- ½ cup dry white wine
- 2 lb squid, sliced into rings
- Salt and black pepper to taste
- ⅓ cup green olives, chopped
- 1 tbsp capers
- 2 tbsp fresh parsley, chopped

Directions:

1. Warm the olive oil in a pot over medium heat. Sauté the onion, garlic, red chili, and celery until softened, about 5 minutes. Stir in pepper flakes and cook for about 30 seconds. Stir in wine, scraping up any browned bits, and cook until nearly evaporated, about 1 minute. Add 1 cup of water and season with salt and pepper. Stir the squid in the pot. Reduce heat to low, cover, and simmer until squid has released its liquid, about 15 minutes. Pour in tomatoes, olives, and capers, and continue to cook until squid is very tender, 30-35 minutes. Top with parsley. Serve and enjoy!

Nutrition Info:

- Info Per Serving: Calories: 334;Fat: 12g;Protein: 28g;Carbs: 30g.

Moules Mariniere (mussels In Wine Sauce)

Servings:4
Cooking Time:15 Minutes
Ingredients:

- 4 tbsp butter
- 4 lb cleaned mussels
- 2 cups dry white wine
- ½ tsp sea salt
- 6 garlic cloves, minced
- 1 shallot, diced
- ½ cup chopped parsley
- Juice of ½ lemon

Directions:

1. Pour the white wine, salt, garlic, shallots, and ¼ cup of the parsley into a large saucepan over medium heat. Cover and bring to boil. Add the mussels and simmer just until all of the mussels open, about 6 minutes. Do not overcook. With a slotted spoon, remove the mussels to a bowl. Add the butter and lemon juice to the saucepan, stir, and pour the broth over the mussels. Garnish with the remaining parsley and serve with a crusty, wholegrain baguette.

Nutrition Info:

- Info Per Serving: Calories: 528;Fat: 24g;Protein: 55g;Carbs: 20g.

Hot Jumbo Shrimp

Servings:4
Cooking Time:20 Minutes
Ingredients:

- 2 lb shell-on jumbo shrimp, deveined
- ¼ cup olive oil
- Salt and black pepper to taste
- 6 garlic cloves, minced
- 1 tsp anise seeds
- ½ tsp red pepper flakes
- 2 tbsp minced fresh cilantro
- 1 lemon, cut into wedges

Directions:

1. Combine the olive oil, garlic, anise seeds, pepper flakes, and black pepper in a large bowl. Add the shrimp and cilantro and toss well, making sure the oil mixture gets into the interior of the shrimp. Arrange shrimp in a single layer on a baking tray. Set under the preheated broiler for approximately 4 minutes. Flip shrimp and continue to broil until it is opaque and shells are beginning to brown, about 2 minutes, rotating sheet halfway through broiling. Serve with lemon wedges.

Nutrition Info:

- Info Per Serving: Calories: 218;Fat: 9g;Protein: 30.8g;Carbs: 2.3g.

Balsamic Asparagus & Salmon Roast

Servings:4
Cooking Time:20 Minutes
Ingredients:

- 2 tbsp olive oil
- 4 salmon fillets, skinless
- 2 tbsp balsamic vinegar
- 1 lb asparagus, trimmed
- Salt and black pepper to taste

Directions:

1. Preheat the oven to 380F. In a roasting pan, arrange the salmon fillets and asparagus spears. Season with salt and pepper and drizzle with olive oil and balsamic vinegar; roast for 12-15 minutes. Serve warm.

Nutrition Info:

- Info Per Serving: Calories: 310;Fat: 16g;Protein: 21g;Carbs: 19g.

Pan-fried Tuna With Vegetables

Servings:4
Cooking Time:25 Minutes
Ingredients:
- 2 tbsp olive oil
- 4 tuna fillets, boneless
- 1 red bell pepper, chopped
- 1 onion, chopped
- 4 garlic cloves, minced
- ½ cup fish stock
- 1 tsp basil, dried
- ½ cup cherry tomatoes, halved
- ½ cup black olives, halved
- Salt and black pepper to taste

Directions:
1. Warm the olive oil in a skillet over medium heat and fry tuna for 10 minutes on both sides. Divide the fish among plates. In the same skillet, cook onion, bell pepper, garlic, and cherry tomatoes for 3 minutes. Stir in salt, pepper, fish stock, basil, and olives and cook for another 3 minutes. Top the tuna with the mixture and serve immediately.

Nutrition Info:
- Info Per Serving: Calories: 260;Fat: 9g;Protein: 29g;Carbs: 6g.

Baked Fish With Pistachio Crust

Servings:4
Cooking Time: 15 To 20 Minutes
Ingredients:
- ½ cup extra-virgin olive oil, divided
- 1 pound flaky white fish (such as cod, haddock, or halibut), skin removed
- ½ cup shelled finely chopped pistachios
- ½ cup ground flaxseed
- Zest and juice of 1 lemon, divided
- 1 teaspoon ground cumin
- 1 teaspoon ground allspice
- ½ teaspoon salt
- ¼ teaspoon freshly ground black pepper

Directions:
1. Preheat the oven to 400ºF.
2. Line a baking sheet with parchment paper or aluminum foil and drizzle 2 tablespoons of olive oil over the sheet, spreading to evenly coat the bottom.
3. Cut the fish into 4 equal pieces and place on the prepared baking sheet.
4. In a small bowl, combine the pistachios, flaxseed, lemon zest, cumin, allspice, salt, and pepper. Drizzle in ¼ cup of olive oil and stir well.
5. Divide the nut mixture evenly on top of the fish pieces. Drizzle the lemon juice and remaining 2 tablespoons of olive oil over the fish and bake until cooked through, 15 to 20 minutes, depending on the thickness of the fish.
6. Cool for 5 minutes before serving.

Nutrition Info:
- Info Per Serving: Calories: 509;Fat: 41.0g;Protein: 26.0g;Carbs: 9.0g.

Gluten-free Almond-crusted Salmon

Servings:4
Cooking Time:20 Minutes
Ingredients:
- 1 tbsp olive oil
- ½ tsp lemon zest
- ¼ cup breadcrumbs
- ½ cup toasted almonds, ground
- ½ tsp dried thyme
- Salt and black pepper to taste
- 4 salmon steaks
- 1 lemon, cut into wedges

Directions:
1. Preheat oven to 350 F. In a shallow dish, combine the lemon zest, breadcrumbs, almonds, thyme, salt, and pepper. Coat the salmon steaks with olive oil and arrange them on a baking sheet. Cover them with the almond mixture, pressing down lightly with your fingers to create a tightly packed crust. Bake for 10-12 minutes or until the almond crust is lightly browned and the fish is cooked through. Serve garnished with lemon wedges.

Nutrition Info:
- Info Per Serving: Calories: 568;Fat: 28g;Protein: 66g;Carbs: 9.6g.

Scallion Clams With Snow Peas

Servings:4
Cooking Time:30 Minutes
Ingredients:
- 2 tbsp olive oil
- 1 tbsp basil, chopped
- 2 lb clams
- 1 onion, chopped
- 4 garlic cloves, minced
- Salt and black pepper to taste
- ½ cup vegetable stock
- 1 cup snow peas, sliced
- ½ tbsp balsamic vinegar
- 1 cup scallions, sliced

Directions:
1. Warm olive oil in a skillet over medium heat. Sauté onion and garlic for 2 to 3 minutes until tender and fragrant, stirring often. Add in the clams, salt, pepper, vegetable stock, snow peas, balsamic vinegar, and basil and bring to a boil. Lower the heat and simmer for 10 minutes. Remove from the heat. Discard any unopened clams. Scatter with scallions.

Nutrition Info:
- Info Per Serving: Calories: 310;Fat: 13g;Protein: 22g;Carbs: 27g.

Poultry And Meats Recipes

Slow Cooker Beef Stew

Servings:4
Cooking Time:8 Hours 10 Minutes
Ingredients:

- 2 tbsp canola oil
- 2 lb beef stew meat, cubed
- Salt and black pepper to taste
- 2 cups beef stock
- 2 shallots, chopped
- 2 tbsp thyme, chopped
- 2 garlic cloves, minced
- 1 carrot, chopped
- 3 celery stalks, chopped
- 28 oz canned tomatoes, diced
- 2 tbsp parsley, chopped

Directions:
1. Place the beef meat, salt, pepper, beef stock, canola oil, shallots, thyme, garlic, carrot, celery, and tomatoes in your slow cooker. Put the lid and cook for 8 hours on Low. Sprinkle with parsley and serve warm.

Nutrition Info:
- Info Per Serving: Calories: 370;Fat: 17g;Protein: 35g;Carbs: 28g.

Spinach Chicken With Chickpeas

Servings:4
Cooking Time:25 Minutes
Ingredients:

- 2 tbsp olive oil
- 1 lb chicken breasts, cubed
- 10 oz spinach, chopped
- 1 cup canned chickpeas
- 1 onion, chopped
- 2 garlic cloves, minced
- ½ cup chicken stock
- 2 tbsp Parmesan cheese, grated
- 1 tbsp parsley, chopped
- Salt and black pepper to taste

Directions:
1. Warm the olive oil in a skillet over medium heat and brown chicken for 5 minutes. Season with salt and pepper. Stir in onion and garlic for 3 minutes. Pour in stock and chickpeas and bring to a boil. Cook for 20 minutes. Mix in spinach and cook until wilted, about 5 minutes. Top with Parmesan cheese and parsley. Serve and enjoy!

Nutrition Info:
- Info Per Serving: Calories: 290;Fat: 10g;Protein: 35g;Carbs: 22g.

Chicken With Halloumi Cheese

Servings:4
Cooking Time:40 Minutes
Ingredients:

- 2 tbsp butter
- 1 cup Halloumi cheese, cubed
- Salt and black pepper to taste
- 1 hard-boiled egg yolk
- ½ cup olive oil
- 6 black olives, halved
- 1 tbsp fresh cilantro, chopped
- 1 tbsp balsamic vinegar
- 1 tbsp garlic, finely minced
- 1 tbsp fresh lemon juice
- 1 ½ lb chicken wings

Directions:

1. Melt the butter in a saucepan over medium heat. Sear the chicken wings for 5 minutes per side. Season with salt and pepper to taste. Place the chicken wings on a parchment-lined baking pan. Mash the egg yolk with a fork and mix in the garlic, lemon juice, balsamic vinegar, olive oil, and salt until creamy, uniform, and smooth.
2. Preheat oven to 380 F. Spread the egg mixture over the chicken. Bake for 15-20 minutes. Top with the cheese and bake an additional 5 minutes until hot and bubbly. Scatter cilantro and olives on top of the chicken wings. Serve.

Nutrition Info:

- Info Per Serving: Calories: 560;Fat: 48g;Protein: 41g;Carbs: 2g.

Dragon Pork Chops With Pickle Topping

Servings:4
Cooking Time:30 Minutes
Ingredients:

- ½ cup roasted bell peppers, chopped
- 6 dill pickles, sliced
- 1 cup dill pickle juice
- 6 pork chops, boneless
- Salt and black pepper to taste
- 1 tsp hot pepper sauce
- 1 ½ cups tomatoes, cubed
- 1 jalapeno pepper, chopped
- 10 black olives, sliced

Directions:

1. Place pork chops, hot sauce, and pickle juice in a bowl and marinate in the fridge for 15 minutes. Preheat your grill to High. Remove the chops from the fridge and grill them for 14 minutes on both sides. Combine dill pickles, tomatoes, jalapeño pepper, roasted peppers, and black olives in a bowl. Serve chops topped with the pickle mixture.

Nutrition Info:

- Info Per Serving: Calories: 230;Fat: 7g;Protein: 36g;Carbs: 7g.

Beef & Pumpkin Stew

Servings:6
Cooking Time:35 Minutes

Ingredients:

- 2 tbsp canola oil
- 2 lb stew beef, cubed
- 1 cup red wine
- 1 onion, chopped
- 1 tsp garlic powder
- Salt to taste
- 3 whole cloves
- 1 bay leaf
- 3 carrots, chopped
- ½ butternut pumpkin, diced
- 2 tbsp cornstarch
- 3 tbsp water

Directions:

1. Warm oil on Sauté mode. Brown the beef for 5 minutes on each side. Deglaze the pot with wine, scrape the bottom to get rid of any browned beef bits. Add in onion, salt, bay leaf, cloves, and garlic powder. Seal the lid, press Meat/Stew and cook on High for 15 minutes. Release the Pressure quickly. Add in pumpkin and carrots without stirring.
2. Seal the lid and cook on High Pressure for 5 minutes. Release the Pressure quickly. In a bowl, mix water and cornstarch until cornstarch dissolves completely; mix into the stew. Allow the stew to simmer while uncovered on Keep Warm for 5 minutes until you attain the desired thickness.

Nutrition Info:

- Info Per Serving: Calories: 340;Fat: 14g;Protein: 34g;Carbs: 12g.

Fennel Beef Ribs

Servings:4
Cooking Time:2 Hours 10 Minutes

Ingredients:

- 2 tbsp olive oil
- 2 lb beef ribs
- 2 garlic cloves, minced
- 1 onion, chopped
- ½ cup chicken stock
- 1 tbsp ground fennel seeds

Directions:

1. Preheat oven to 360 F. Mix garlic, onion, stock, olive oil, fennel seeds, and beef ribs in a roasting pan and bake for 2 hours. Serve hot with salad.

Nutrition Info:

- Info Per Serving: Calories: 300;Fat: 10g;Protein: 25g;Carbs: 18g.

Citrus Chicken Wings

Servings:6
Cooking Time:50 Minutes

Ingredients:

- 2 tbsp canola oils
- 12 chicken wings, halved
- 2 garlic cloves, minced
- 1 lime, juiced and zested
- 1 cup raisins, soaked
- 1 tsp cumin, ground
- Salt and black pepper to taste
- ½ cup chicken stock
- 1 tbsp chives, chopped

Directions:

1. Preheat the oven to 340 F. Combine chicken wings, garlic, lime juice, lime zest, canola oil, raisins, cumin, salt, pepper, stock, and chives in a baking pan. Bake for 40 minutes.

Nutrition Info:

- Info Per Serving: Calories: 300;Fat: 20g;Protein: 19g;Carbs: 22g.

Nutty Chicken Breasts

Servings:4
Cooking Time:65 Minutes
Ingredients:

- 2 tbsp canola oil
- 1 lb chicken breasts, halved
- ½ tsp hot paprika
- 1 cup chicken stock
- 2 tbsp hazelnuts, chopped
- 2 spring onions, chopped
- 2 garlic cloves, minced
- ¼ cup Parmesan cheese, grated
- 2 tbsp cilantro, chopped
- 2 tbsp parsley, chopped
- Salt and black pepper to taste

Directions:

1. Preheat the oven to 370 F. Combine chicken, canola oil, hot paprika, stock, hazelnuts, spring onions, garlic, salt, and pepper in a greased baking pan and bake for 40 minutes. Sprinkle with Parmesan cheese and bake for an additional 5 minutes until the cheese melts. Top with cilantro and parsley.

Nutrition Info:

- Info Per Serving: Calories: 230;Fat: 10g;Protein: 19g;Carbs: 22g.

Tomato Caper & Turkey Pot

Servings:4
Cooking Time:8 Hours 10 Minutes
Ingredients:

- 2 tbsp capers, drained
- 1 lb turkey breast, sliced
- 2 cups canned tomatoes, diced
- 2 garlic cloves, minced
- 1 yellow onion, chopped
- 2 cups chicken stock
- ¼ cup rosemary, chopped
- Salt and black pepper to taste

Directions:

1. Place turkey, tomatoes, garlic, onion, chicken stock, capers, rosemary, salt, and pepper in your slow cooker. Cover with the lid and cook for 8 hours on Low. Serve warm.

Nutrition Info:

- Info Per Serving: Calories: 300;Fat: 10g;Protein: 38g;Carbs: 26g.

Asparagus & Chicken Skillet

Servings:4
Cooking Time:30 Minutes
Ingredients:

- 2 tbsp olive oil
- 1 lb chicken breasts, sliced
- Salt and black pepper to taste
- 1 lb asparagus, chopped
- 6 sundried tomatoes, diced
- 3 tbsp capers, drained
- 2 tbsp lemon juice

Directions:

1. Warm the olive oil in a skillet over medium heat. Cook asparagus, tomatoes, salt, pepper, capers, and lemon juice for 10 minutes. Remove to a bowl. Brown chicken in the same skillet for 8 minutes on both sides. Put veggies back to skillet and cook for another 2-3 minutes. Serve and enjoy!

Nutrition Info:

- Info Per Serving: Calories: 560;Fat: 29g;Protein: 45g;Carbs: 34g.

Easy Pork Stew

Servings:4
Cooking Time:50 Minutes
Ingredients:

- 1 tbsp olive oil
- 1 lb pork stew meat, cubed
- 2 shallots, chopped
- 14 oz canned tomatoes, diced
- 1 garlic clove, minced
- 3 cups beef stock
- 2 tbsp paprika
- 1 tsp coriander seeds
- 1 tsp dried thyme
- Salt and black pepper to taste
- 2 tbsp parsley, chopped

Directions:

1. Warm the olive oil in a pot over medium heat and cook pork meat for 5 minutes until brown, stirring occasionally. Add in shallots and garlic and cook for an additional 3 minutes. Stir in beef stock, tomatoes, paprika, thyme, coriander seeds, salt, and pepper and bring to a boil; cook for 30 minutes. Serve warm topped with parsley.

Nutrition Info:

- Info Per Serving: Calories: 330;Fat: 18g;Protein: 35g;Carbs: 28g.

Bell Pepper & Olive Turkey Breasts

Servings:4
Cooking Time:70 Minutes
Ingredients:

- 4 mixed bell peppers, chopped
- 1 lb turkey breast strips
- 2 leeks, chopped
- 4 garlic cloves, minced
- ½ cup black olives, sliced
- 2 cups chicken stock
- 1 tbsp oregano, chopped
- ½ cup cilantro, chopped

Directions:

1. Preheat the oven to 380 F. Put leeks, bell peppers, garlic, olives, stock, turkey, oregano, and cilantro in a baking pan and roast for 1 hour. Serve right away.

Nutrition Info:

- Info Per Serving: Calories: 240;Fat: 10g;Protein: 35g;Carbs: 19g.

Baked Peppery Parsnip & Pork

Servings:4
Cooking Time:90 Minutes
Ingredients:

- 2 tbsp olive oil
- 2 lb pork loin, sliced
- 2 parsnips, chopped
- 5 black peppercorns, crushed
- 2 red onions, chopped
- 2 cups Greek yogurt
- 1 tsp mustard
- Salt and black pepper to taste

Directions:

1. Preheat oven to 360 F. Warm the olive oil in a skillet over medium heat and sear pork for 8 minutes on all sides. Remove to a bowl. In the same skillet, cook onions, parsnips, and peppercorns and cook for 5 minutes. Put the pork back along with the yogurt, mustard, salt, and pepper. Bake for 1 hour.

Nutrition Info:

- Info Per Serving: Calories: 230;Fat: 8g;Protein: 16g;Carbs: 22g.

Grilled Pork Chops With Apricot Chutney

Servings:4
Cooking Time:40 Minutes
Ingredients:

- 1 tbsp olive oil
- ½ tsp garlic powder
- 4 pork loin chops, boneless
- Salt and black pepper to taste
- ¼ tsp ground cumin
- ½ tsp sage, dried
- 1 tsp chili powder
- For the chutney

- 3 cups apricots, peeled and chopped
- ½ cup red sweet pepper, chopped
- 1 tsp olive oil
- ¼ cup shallot, minced
- ½ jalapeno pepper, minced
- 1 tbsp balsamic vinegar
- 2 tbsp cilantro, chopped

Directions:

1. Warm the olive oil in a skillet over medium heat and cook the shallot for 5 minutes. Stir in sweet pepper, apricots, jalapeño pepper, vinegar, and cilantro and cook for 10 minutes. Remove from heat.
2. In the meantime, sprinkle pork chops with olive oil, salt, pepper, garlic powder, cumin, sage, and chili powder. Preheat the grill to medium heat. Grill pork chops for 12-14 minutes on both sides. Serve topped with apricot chutney.

Nutrition Info:

- Info Per Serving: Calories: 300;Fat: 11g;Protein: 39g;Carbs: 14g.

Tomato & Basil Chicken Breasts

Servings:4
Cooking Time:30 Minutes
Ingredients:

- 2 tbsp olive oil
- 1 lb chicken breasts
- ½ tsp garlic powder
- ¼ tsp chili powder
- Salt and black pepper to taste
- 1 large tomato, sliced thinly
- 1 cup mozzarella, shredded
- 1 can diced tomatoes
- 2 tbsp fresh basil leaves, torn
- 4 tsp balsamic vinegar

Directions:

1. Preheat oven to 450 F. Flatten the chicken breasts with a rolling pin. Add the chicken, olive oil, garlic powder, chili powder, black pepper, and salt to a resealable bag. Seal the bag and massage the ingredients into the chicken. Take the chicken out of the bag and place it on a greased baking sheet.
2. Bake the chicken for 15-18 minutes or until the meat reaches an internal temperature of 160 F and the juices run clear. Layer the tomato slices on each chicken breast and top with mozzarella cheese. Broil the chicken for another 2-3 minutes or until the cheese melts. Remove the chicken from the oven. Microwave the crushed tomatoes for 1 minute. Divide the tomatoes between plates and top with chicken breasts. Scatter with basil and a drizzle of balsamic vinegar.

Nutrition Info:

- Info Per Serving: Calories: 258;Fat: 10g;Protein: 14g;Carbs: 28g.

Drunken Lamb Bake

Servings:4

Cooking Time:90 Minutes

Ingredients:

- 3 tbsp butter
- 2 lb leg of lamb, sliced
- 3 garlic cloves, chopped
- 2 onions, chopped
- 3 cups vegetable stock
- 2 cups dry red wine
- 2 tbsp tomato pastes
- 1 tsp thyme, chopped
- Salt and black pepper to taste

Directions:

1. Preheat the oven to 360 F. Melt butter in a skillet over medium heat. Sear lamb for 10 minutes on both sides. Remove to a roasting pan. In the same skillet, add and cook onions and garlic for 5 minutes. Stir in stock, red wine, tomato paste, thyme, salt, and pepper and bring to a boil. Cook for 10 minutes and pour over lamb. Bake for 1 hour.

Nutrition Info:

- Info Per Serving: Calories: 290;Fat: 22g;Protein: 19g;Carbs: 17g.

Grilled Lemon Chicken

Servings:2

Cooking Time: 12 To 14 Minutes

Ingredients:

- Marinade:
- 4 tablespoons freshly squeezed lemon juice
- 2 tablespoons olive oil, plus more for greasing the grill grates
- 1 teaspoon dried basil
- 1 teaspoon paprika
- ½ teaspoon dried thyme
- ¼ teaspoon salt
- ¼ teaspoon garlic powder
- 2 boneless, skinless chicken breasts

Directions:

1. Make the marinade: Whisk together the lemon juice, olive oil, basil, paprika, thyme, salt, and garlic powder in a large bowl until well combined.

2. Add the chicken breasts to the bowl and let marinate for at least 30 minutes.

3. When ready to cook, preheat the grill to medium-high heat. Lightly grease the grill grates with the olive oil.

4. Discard the marinade and arrange the chicken breasts on the grill grates.

5. Grill for 12 to 14 minutes, flipping the chicken halfway through, or until a meat thermometer inserted in the center of the chicken reaches 165°F.

6. Let the chicken cool for 5 minutes and serve warm.

Nutrition Info:

- Info Per Serving: Calories: 251;Fat: 15.5g;Protein: 27.3g;Carbs: 1.9g.

Lamb Tagine With Couscous And Almonds

Servings:6
Cooking Time: 7 Hours 7 Minutes
Ingredients:

- 2 tablespoons almond flour
- Juice and zest of 1 navel orange
- 2 tablespoons extra-virgin olive oil
- 2 pounds boneless lamb leg, fat trimmed and cut into 1½-inch cubes
- ½ cup low-sodium chicken stock
- 2 large white onions, chopped
- 1 teaspoon pumpkin pie spice
- ¼ teaspoon crushed saffron threads
- 1 teaspoon ground cumin
- ¼ teaspoon ground red pepper flakes
- ½ teaspoon sea salt
- 2 tablespoons raw honey
- 1 cup pitted dates
- 3 cups cooked couscous, for serving
- 2 tablespoons toasted slivered almonds, for serving

Directions:
1. Combine the almond flour with orange juice in a large bowl. Stir until smooth, then mix in the orange zest. Set aside.
2. Heat the olive oil in a nonstick skillet over medium-high heat until shimmering.
3. Add the lamb cubes and sauté for 7 minutes or until lightly browned.
4. Pour in the flour mixture and chicken stock, then add the onions, pumpkin pie spice, saffron, cumin, ground red pepper flakes, and salt. Stir to mix well.
5. Pour them in the slow cooker. Cover and cook on low for 6 hours or until the internal temperature of the lamb reaches at least 145ºF.
6. When the cooking is complete, mix in the honey and dates, then cook for another an hour.
7. Put the couscous in a tagine bowl or a simple large bowl, then top with lamb mixture. Scatter with slivered almonds and serve immediately.

Nutrition Info:
- Info Per Serving: Calories: 447;Fat: 10.2g;Protein: 36.3g;Carbs: 53.5g.

Simple Chicken With Olive Tapenade

Servings:4
Cooking Time:35 Minutes
Ingredients:

- ½ cup olive oil
- 2 tbsp capers, canned
- 2 chicken breasts
- 1 cup black olives, pitted
- Salt and black pepper to taste
- ½ cup parsley, chopped
- ½ cup rosemary, chopped
- Salt and black pepper to taste
- 2 garlic cloves, minced
- ½ lemon, juiced and zested

Directions:
1. In a food processor, blend olives, capers, half of the oil, salt, pepper, parsley, rosemary, garlic, lemon zest, and lemon juice until smooth; set aside. Warm the remaining oil in a skillet over medium heat. Brown the chicken for 8-10 minutes on both sides. Top with tapenade. Serve and enjoy!

Nutrition Info:
- Info Per Serving: Calories: 300;Fat: 14g;Protein: 35g;Carbs: 17g.

Parsley Eggplant Lamb

Servings:4
Cooking Time:70 Minutes
Ingredients:
- 2 tbsp olive oil
- 1 cup chicken stock
- 1 ½ lb lamb meat, cubed
- 2 eggplants, cubed
- 2 onions, chopped
- 2 tbsp tomato paste
- 2 tbsp parsley, chopped
- 4 garlic cloves, minced

Directions:

1. Warm the olive oil in a skillet over medium heat and cook onions and garlic for 4 minutes. Put in lamb and cook for 6 minutes. Stir in eggplants and tomato paste for 5 minutes. Pour in the stock and bring to a boil. Cook for another 50 minutes, stirring often. Serve garnished with parsley.

Nutrition Info:
- Info Per Serving: Calories: 310;Fat: 19g;Protein: 15g;Carbs: 23g.

Eggplant & Turkey Moussaka

Servings:4
Cooking Time:55 Minutes
Ingredients:
- 5 tbsp olive oil
- 1 lb ground turkey
- 1 can diced tomatoes
- 1 cup Greek yogurt
- 2 small eggplants, sliced
- 2 shallots, chopped
- 2 garlic cloves, minced
- 2 tbsp tomato paste
- 1 tsp dried oregano
- 1 egg, beaten
- Salt and black pepper to taste
- ¼ tsp ground coriander
- 2 oz grated Halloumi cheese
- 2 tbsp chopped fresh parsley

Directions:

1. Preheat oven to 400 F. Warm olive oil in a pan over medium heat and cook the eggplant slices for 6-8 minutes on both sides. Remove to paper towels. In the same pan, sauté shallots and garlic for 3 minutes, stirring often. Add in ground turkey and cook for 5 minutes until no longer pink. Stir in tomato paste, tomatoes, oregano, ground coriander, salt, and pepper; cook for 4-5 minutes.

2. Combine yogurt, egg, salt, and pepper in a bowl. Spread half of the turkey mixture on a baking dish, add a layer of eggplant, then remaining meat, and finally remaining eggplants. Bake for 15 minutes. Remove and top with the yogurt mixture. Sprinkle with the cheese and return in the oven for 5-8 minutes until the cheese melts. Top with parsley.

Nutrition Info:
- Info Per Serving: Calories: 521;Fat: 33g;Protein: 42g;Carbs: 23g.

Chicken Thighs Al Orange

Servings:4
Cooking Time:40 Minutes
Ingredients:

- 2 tbsp olive oil
- 2 tbsp sweet chili sauce
- 2 lb chicken thighs, cubed
- Salt and black pepper to taste
- 1 ½ tsp orange extract
- ¼ cup orange juice
- 2 tbsp cilantro, chopped
- 1 cup chicken stock
- ¼ tsp red pepper flakes
- 2 cups cooked white rice

Directions:

1. Warm the olive oil in a skillet over medium heat and sear chicken for 8 minutes on all sides. Season with salt and pepper and stir in orange extract, orange juice, stock, sweet chili sauce, and red pepper flakes. Bring to a boil. Cook for 20 minutes. Top with cilantro and serve over cooked rice.

Nutrition Info:

- Info Per Serving: Calories: 310;Fat: 15g;Protein: 26g;Carbs: 23g.

Tasty Chicken Pot

Servings:4
Cooking Time:35 Minutes
Ingredients:

- 1 lb chicken thighs, skinless and boneless
- 2 tbsp olive oil
- 1 onion, chopped
- 2 garlic cloves, minced
- 1 tsp smoked paprika
- 1 tsp chili powder
- ½ tsp fennel seeds, ground
- 2 tsp oregano, dried
- 14 oz canned tomatoes, diced
- ½ cup capers

Directions:

1. Warm the olive oil in a skillet over medium heat and sauté the onion, garlic, paprika, chili powder, fennel seeds, and oregano for 3 minutes. Put in chicken, tomatoes, 1 cup of water, and capers. Bring to a boil and simmer for 20-25 minutes.

Nutrition Info:

- Info Per Serving: Calories: 160;Fat: 9g;Protein: 13g;Carbs: 10g.

Stewed Chicken Sausage With Farro

Servings:2
Cooking Time:55 Minutes
Ingredients:

- 8 oz hot Italian chicken sausage, removed from the casing
- 1 tbsp olive oil
- ½ onion, diced
- 1 garlic clove, minced
- 8 sundried tomatoes, diced
- ½ cup farro
- 1 cup chicken stock
- 2 cups arugula
- 5 fresh basil, sliced thin

Directions:

1. Warm the olive oil in a pan over medium heat. Sauté the onion and garlic for 5 minutes. Add the sun-dried tomatoes and chicken sausage, stirring to break up the sausage. Cook for 7 minutes or until the sausage is no longer pink. Stir in the farro for about 2 minutes. Add the chicken stock and bring the mixture to a boil. Cover the pan and reduce the heat to low. Simmer for 30 minutes or until the farro is tender. Stir in arugula and let it wilt slightly, 2 minutes. Sprinkle with basil and serve.

Nutrition Info:

- Info Per Serving: Calories: 491;Fat: 19g;Protein: 31g;Carbs: 53g.

Deluxe Chicken With Yogurt Sauce

Servings:4
Cooking Time:40 Minutes

Ingredients:

- 2 tbsp olive oil
- 1/3 cup Greek yogurt
- 1 lb chicken breasts, halved
- 2 garlic cloves, minced
- 2 tbsp lemon juice
- 1 tbsp red wine vinegar
- 2 tbsp dill, chopped
- Salt and black pepper to taste

Directions:

1. Preheat the oven to 380 F. In a food processor, blend garlic, lemon juice, vinegar, yogurt, dill, salt, and pepper until smooth. Warm olive oil in a skillet over medium heat. Sear chicken for 6 minutes on both sides. Pour yogurt sauce over chicken and bake for 25 minutes. Serve.

Nutrition Info:

- Info Per Serving: Calories: 290;Fat: 13g;Protein: 15g;Carbs: 19g.

Pork Millet With Chestnuts

Servings:6
Cooking Time:30 Minutes

Ingredients:

- 2 cups pork roast, cooked and shredded
- ½ cup sour cream
- 1 cup millet
- 3 oz water chestnuts, sliced
- Salt and white pepper to taste

Directions:

1. Place millet and salted water in a pot over medium heat and cook for 20 minutes. Drain and remove to a bowl to cool. When ready, add in pork, chestnuts, cream, salt, and pepper and mix to combine. Serve.

Nutrition Info:

- Info Per Serving: Calories: 300;Fat: 18g;Protein: 24g;Carbs: 17g.

Vegetable Mains And Meatless Recipes

Braised Cauliflower With White Wine

Servings:4
Cooking Time: 12 To 16 Minutes
Ingredients:

- 3 tablespoons plus 1 teaspoon extra-virgin olive oil, divided
- 3 garlic cloves, minced
- ⅛ teaspoon red pepper flakes
- 1 head cauliflower, cored and cut into 1½-inch florets
- ¼ teaspoon salt, plus more for seasoning
- Black pepper, to taste
- ⅓ cup vegetable broth
- ⅓ cup dry white wine
- 2 tablespoons minced fresh parsley

Directions:

1. Combine 1 teaspoon of the oil, garlic and pepper flakes in small bowl.
2. Heat the remaining 3 tablespoons of the oil in a skillet over medium-high heat until shimmering. Add the cauliflower and ¼ teaspoon of the salt and cook for 7 to 9 minutes, stirring occasionally, or until florets are golden brown.
3. Push the cauliflower to sides of the skillet. Add the garlic mixture to the center of the skillet. Cook for about 30 seconds, or until fragrant. Stir the garlic mixture into the cauliflower.
4. Pour in the broth and wine and bring to simmer. Reduce the heat to medium-low. Cover and cook for 4 to 6 minutes, or until the cauliflower is crisp-tender. Off heat, stir in the parsley and season with salt and pepper.
5. Serve immediately.

Nutrition Info:

- Info Per Serving: Calories: 143;Fat: 11.7g;Protein: 3.1g;Carbs: 8.7g.

Feta & Zucchini Rosti Cakes

Servings:4
Cooking Time:25 Minutes
Ingredients:

- 5 tbsp olive oil
- 1 lb zucchini, shredded
- 4 spring onions, chopped
- Salt and black pepper to taste
- 4 oz feta cheese, crumbled
- 1 egg, lightly beaten
- 2 tbsp minced fresh dill
- 1 garlic clove, minced
- ¼ cup flour
- Lemon wedges for serving

Directions:

1. Preheat oven to 380 F. In a large bowl, mix the zucchini, spring onions, feta cheese, egg, dill, garlic, salt, and pepper. Sprinkle flour over the mixture and stir to incorporate.
2. Warm the oil in a skillet over medium heat. Cook the rosti mixture in small flat fritters for about 4 minutes per side until crisp and golden on both sides, pressing with a fish slice as they cook. Serve with lemon wedges.

Nutrition Info:

- Info Per Serving: Calories: 239;Fat: 19.8g;Protein: 7.8g;Carbs: 9g.

Tasty Lentil Burgers

Servings:4
Cooking Time:25 Minutes
Ingredients:

- 1 cup cremini mushrooms, finely chopped
- 1 cup cooked green lentils
- ½ cup Greek yogurt
- ½ lemon, zested and juiced
- ½ tsp garlic powder
- ½ tsp dried oregano
- 1 tbsp fresh cilantro, chopped
- Salt to taste
- 3 tbsp extra-virgin olive oil
- ¼ tsp tbsp white miso
- ¼ tsp smoked paprika
- ¼ cup flour

Directions:

1. Pour ½ cup of lentils in your blender and puree partially until somewhat smooth, but with many whole lentils still remaining. In a small bowl, mix the yogurt, lemon zest and juice, garlic powder, oregano, cilantro, and salt. Season and set aside. In a medium bowl, mix the mushrooms, 2 tablespoons of olive oil, miso, and paprika. Stir in all the lentils. Add in flour and stir until the mixture everything is well incorporated. Shape the mixture into patties about ¾-inch thick. Warm the remaining olive oil in a skillet over medium heat. Fry the patties until browned and crisp, about 3 minutes. Turn and fry on the second side. Serve with the reserved yogurt mixture.

Nutrition Info:

- Info Per Serving: Calories: 215;Fat: 13g;Protein: 10g;Carbs: 19g.

Vegan Lentil Bolognese

Servings:2
Cooking Time: 50 Minutes
Ingredients:

- 1 medium celery stalk
- 1 large carrot
- ½ large onion
- 1 garlic clove
- 2 tablespoons olive oil
- 1 can crushed tomatoes
- 1 cup red wine
- ½ teaspoon salt, plus more as needed
- ½ teaspoon pure maple syrup
- 1 cup cooked lentils (prepared from ½ cup dry)

Directions:

1. Add the celery, carrot, onion, and garlic to a food processor and process until everything is finely chopped.
2. In a Dutch oven, heat the olive oil over medium-high heat. Add the chopped mixture and sauté for about 10 minutes, stirring occasionally, or until the vegetables are lightly browned.
3. Stir in the tomatoes, wine, salt, and maple syrup and bring to a boil.
4. Once the sauce starts to boil, cover, and reduce the heat to medium-low. Simmer for 30 minutes, stirring occasionally, or until the vegetables are softened.
5. Stir in the cooked lentils and cook for an additional 5 minutes until warmed through.
6. Taste and add additional salt, if needed. Serve warm.

Nutrition Info:

- Info Per Serving: Calories: 367;Fat: 15.0g;Protein: 13.7g;Carbs: 44.5g.

Cheesy Sweet Potato Burgers

Servings:4

Cooking Time: 19 To 20 Minutes

Ingredients:

- 1 large sweet potato
- 2 tablespoons extra-virgin olive oil, divided
- 1 cup chopped onion
- 1 large egg
- 1 garlic clove
- 1 cup old-fashioned rolled oats
- 1 tablespoon dried oregano
- 1 tablespoon balsamic vinegar
- ¼ teaspoon kosher salt
- ½ cup crumbled Gorgonzola cheese

Directions:

1. Using a fork, pierce the sweet potato all over and microwave on high for 4 to 5 minutes, until softened in the center. Cool slightly before slicing in half.

2. Meanwhile, in a large skillet over medium-high heat, heat 1 tablespoon of the olive oil. Add the onion and sauté for 5 minutes.

3. Spoon the sweet potato flesh out of the skin and put the flesh in a food processor. Add the cooked onion, egg, garlic, oats, oregano, vinegar and salt. Pulse until smooth. Add the cheese and pulse four times to barely combine.

4. Form the mixture into four burgers. Place the burgers on a plate, and press to flatten each to about ¾-inch thick.

5. Wipe out the skillet with a paper towel. Heat the remaining 1 tablespoon of the oil over medium-high heat for about 2 minutes. Add the burgers to the hot oil, then reduce the heat to medium. Cook the burgers for 5 minutes per side.

6. Transfer the burgers to a plate and serve.

Nutrition Info:

- Info Per Serving: Calories: 290;Fat: 12.0g;Protein: 12.0g;Carbs: 43.0g.

Baked Vegetable Stew

Servings:6

Cooking Time:70 Minutes

Ingredients:

- 1 can diced tomatoes, drained with juice reserved
- 3 tbsp olive oil
- 1 onion, chopped
- 2 tbsp fresh oregano, minced
- 1 tsp paprika
- 4 garlic cloves, minced
- 1 ½ lb green beans, sliced
- 1 lb Yukon Gold potatoes, peeled and chopped
- 1 tbsp tomato paste
- Salt and black pepper to taste
- 3 tbsp fresh basil, chopped

Directions:

1. Preheat oven to 360 F. Warm the olive oil in a skillet over medium heat. Sauté onion and garlic for 3 minutes until softened. Stir in oregano and paprika for 30 seconds. Transfer to a baking dish and add in green beans, potatoes, tomatoes, tomato paste, salt, pepper, and 1 ½ cups of water; stir well. Bake for 40-50 minutes. Sprinkle with basil. Serve.

Nutrition Info:

- Info Per Serving: Calories: 121;Fat: 0.8g;Protein: 4.2g;Carbs: 26g.

Garlicky Zucchini Cubes With Mint

Servings:4
Cooking Time: 10 Minutes
Ingredients:

- 3 large green zucchinis, cut into ½-inch cubes
- 3 tablespoons extra-virgin olive oil
- 1 large onion, chopped
- 3 cloves garlic, minced
- 1 teaspoon salt
- 1 teaspoon dried mint

Directions:

1. Heat the olive oil in a large skillet over medium heat.
2. Add the onion and garlic and sauté for 3 minutes, stirring constantly, or until softened.
3. Stir in the zucchini cubes and salt and cook for 5 minutes, or until the zucchini is browned and tender.
4. Add the mint to the skillet and toss to combine, then continue cooking for 2 minutes.
5. Serve warm.

Nutrition Info:

- Info Per Serving: Calories: 146;Fat: 10.6g;Protein: 4.2g;Carbs: 11.8g.

Balsamic Cherry Tomatoes

Servings:4
Cooking Time:10 Minutes
Ingredients:

- 2 tbsp olive oil
- 2 lb cherry tomatoes, halved
- 2 tbsp balsamic glaze
- Salt and black pepper to taste
- 1 garlic clove, minced
- 2 tbsp fresh basil, torn

Directions:

1. Warm the olive oil in a skillet over medium heat. Add the cherry tomatoes and cook for 1-2 minutes, stirring occasionally. Stir in garlic, salt, and pepper and cook until fragrant, about 30 seconds. Drizzle with balsamic glaze and decorate with basil. Serve and enjoy!

Nutrition Info:

- Info Per Serving: Calories: 45;Fat: 2.5g;Protein: 1.1g;Carbs: 5.6g.

Paprika Cauliflower Steaks With Walnut Sauce

Servings:2

Cooking Time: 30 Minutes

Ingredients:

- Walnut Sauce:
- ½ cup raw walnut halves
- 2 tablespoons virgin olive oil, divided
- 1 clove garlic, chopped
- 1 small yellow onion, chopped
- ½ cup unsweetened almond milk
- 2 tablespoons fresh lemon juice
- Salt and pepper, to taste
- Paprika Cauliflower:
- 1 medium head cauliflower
- 1 teaspoon sweet paprika
- 1 teaspoon minced fresh thyme leaves

Directions:

1. Preheat the oven to 350ºF.

2. Make the walnut sauce: Toast the walnuts in a large, ovenproof skillet over medium heat until fragrant and slightly darkened, about 5 minutes. Transfer the walnuts to a blender.

3. Heat 1 tablespoon of olive oil in the skillet. Add the garlic and onion and sauté for about 2 minutes, or until slightly softened. Transfer the garlic and onion into the blender, along with the almond milk, lemon juice, salt, and pepper. Blend the ingredients until smooth and creamy. Keep the sauce warm while you prepare the cauliflower.

4. Make the paprika cauliflower: Cut two 1-inch-thick "steaks" from the center of the cauliflower. Lightly moisten the steaks with water and season both sides with paprika, thyme, salt, and pepper.

5. Heat the remaining 1 tablespoon of olive oil in the skillet over medium-high heat. Add the cauliflower steaks and sear for about 3 minutes until evenly browned. Flip the cauliflower steaks and transfer the skillet to the oven.

6. Roast in the preheated oven for about 20 minutes until crisp-tender.

7. Serve the cauliflower steaks warm with the walnut sauce on the side.

Nutrition Info:

- Info Per Serving: Calories: 367;Fat: 27.9g;Protein: 7.0g;Carbs: 22.7g.

Zoodles With Walnut Pesto

Servings:4

Cooking Time: 10 Minutes

Ingredients:

- 4 medium zucchinis, spiralized
- ¼ cup extra-virgin olive oil, divided
- 1 teaspoon minced garlic, divided
- ½ teaspoon crushed red pepper
- ¼ teaspoon freshly ground black pepper, divided
- ¼ teaspoon kosher salt, divided
- 2 tablespoons grated Parmesan cheese, divided
- 1 cup packed fresh basil leaves
- ¾ cup walnut pieces, divided

Directions:

1. In a large bowl, stir together the zoodles, 1 tablespoon of the olive oil, ½ teaspoon of the minced garlic, red pepper, ⅛ teaspoon of the black pepper and ⅛ teaspoon of the salt. Set aside.

2. Heat ½ tablespoon of the oil in a large skillet over medium-high heat. Add half of the zoodles to the skillet and cook for 5 minutes, stirring constantly. Transfer the cooked zoodles into a bowl. Repeat with another ½ tablespoon of the oil and the remaining zoodles. When done, add the cooked zoodles to the bowl.

3. Make the pesto: In a food processor, combine the remaining ½ teaspoon of the minced garlic, ⅛ teaspoon of the black pepper and ⅛ teaspoon of the salt, 1 tablespoon of the Parmesan, basil leaves and ¼ cup of the walnuts. Pulse until smooth and then slowly drizzle the remaining 2 tablespoons of the oil into the pesto. Pulse again until well combined.

4. Add the pesto to the zoodles along with the remaining 1 tablespoon of the Parmesan and the remaining ½ cup of the walnuts. Toss to coat well.

5. Serve immediately.

Nutrition Info:

- Info Per Serving: Calories: 166;Fat: 16.0g;Protein: 4.0g;Carbs: 3.0g.

Beet And Watercress Salad

Servings:4
Cooking Time: 8 Minutes

Ingredients:

- 2 pounds beets, scrubbed, trimmed and cut into ¾-inch pieces
- ½ cup water
- 1 teaspoon caraway seeds
- ½ teaspoon table salt, plus more for seasoning
- 1 cup plain Greek yogurt
- 1 small garlic clove, minced
- 5 ounces watercress, torn into bite-size pieces
- 1 tablespoon extra-virgin olive oil, divided, plus more for drizzling
- 1 tablespoon white wine vinegar, divided
- Black pepper, to taste
- 1 teaspoon grated orange zest
- 2 tablespoons orange juice
- ¼ cup coarsely chopped fresh dill
- ¼ cup hazelnuts, toasted, skinned and chopped
- Coarse sea salt, to taste

Directions:

1. Combine the beets, water, caraway seeds and table salt in the Instant Pot. Set the lid in place. Select the Manual mode and set the cooking time for 8 minutes on High Pressure. When the timer goes off, do a quick pressure release.
2. Carefully open the lid. Using a slotted spoon, transfer the beets to a plate. Set aside to cool slightly.
3. In a small bowl, combine the yogurt, garlic and 3 tablespoons of the beet cooking liquid. In a large bowl, toss the watercress with 2 teaspoons of the oil and 1 teaspoon of the vinegar. Season with table salt and pepper.
4. Spread the yogurt mixture over a serving dish. Arrange the watercress on top of the yogurt mixture, leaving 1-inch border of the yogurt mixture.
5. Add the beets to now-empty large bowl and toss with the orange zest and juice, the remaining 2 teaspoons of the vinegar and the remaining 1 teaspoon of the oil. Season with table salt and pepper.
6. Arrange the beets on top of the watercress mixture. Drizzle with the olive oil and sprinkle with the dill, hazelnuts and sea salt.
7. Serve immediately.

Nutrition Info:

- Info Per Serving: Calories: 240;Fat: 15.0g;Protein: 9.0g;Carbs: 19.0g.

Mushroom Filled Zucchini Boats

Servings:2
Cooking Time:50 Minutes

Ingredients:

- 2 zucchini, cut in half lengthwise
- 2 cups button mushrooms, chopped
- 2 tbsp olive oil
- 2 cloves garlic, minced
- 2 tbsp chicken broth
- ¼ tsp dried thyme
- 1 tbsp parsley, finely chopped
- 1 tbsp Italian seasoning
- Salt and black pepper to taste

Directions:

1. Preheat oven to 350 F. Warm the olive oil in a large skillet over medium heat and add the olive oil. Sauté the mushrooms and garlic for 4-5 minutes until tender. Pour in the chicken broth and cook for another 3–4 minutes. Add the parsley, oregano, and Italian seasoning and season with salt and pepper. Stir and remove from the heat. Spoon the mixture into the zucchini halves. Place them in a casserole dish and pour 2-3 tbsp of water or broth in the bottom. Cover with foil and bake for 30-40 minutes until zucchini is tender.

Nutrition Info:

- Info Per Serving: Calories: 165;Fat: 13.9g;Protein: 3.8g;Carbs: 8g.

Baked Honey Acorn Squash

Servings:4
Cooking Time:35 Minutes
Ingredients:

- 1 acorn squash, cut into wedges
- 2 tbsp olive oil
- 2 tbsp honey
- 2 tbsp rosemary, chopped
- 2 tbsp walnuts, chopped

Directions:

1. Preheat oven to 400 F. In a bowl, mix honey, rosemary, and olive oil. Lay the squash wedges on a baking sheet and drizzle with the honey mixture. Bake for 30 minutes until squash is tender and slightly caramelized, turning each slice over halfway through. Serve cooled sprinkled with walnuts.

Nutrition Info:

- Info Per Serving: Calories: 136;Fat: 6g;Protein: 0.9g;Carbs: 20g.

Rainbow Vegetable Kebabs

Servings:4
Cooking Time:30 Minutes
Ingredients:

- 1 cup mushrooms, cut into quarters
- 6 mixed bell peppers, cut into squares
- 4 red onions, cut into 6 wedges
- 4 zucchini, cut into half-moons
- 2 tomatoes, cut into quarters
- 3 tbsp herbed oil

Directions:

1. Preheat your grill to medium-high. Alternate the vegetables onto bamboo skewers. Grill them for 5 minutes on each side until the vegetables begin to char. Remove them from heat and drizzle with herbed oil.

Nutrition Info:

- Info Per Serving: Calories: 238;Fat: 12g;Protein: 6g;Carbs: 34.2g.

Wilted Dandelion Greens With Sweet Onion

Servings:4
Cooking Time: 15 Minutes
Ingredients:

- 1 tablespoon extra-virgin olive oil
- 2 garlic cloves, minced
- 1 Vidalia onion, thinly sliced
- ½ cup low-sodium vegetable broth
- 2 bunches dandelion greens, roughly chopped
- Freshly ground black pepper, to taste

Directions:

1. Heat the olive oil in a large skillet over low heat.
2. Add the garlic and onion and cook for 2 to 3 minutes, stirring occasionally, or until the onion is translucent.
3. Fold in the vegetable broth and dandelion greens and cook for 5 to 7 minutes until wilted, stirring frequently.
4. Sprinkle with the black pepper and serve on a plate while warm.

Nutrition Info:

- Info Per Serving: Calories: 81;Fat: 3.9g;Protein: 3.2g;Carbs: 10.8g.

Roasted Vegetables And Chickpeas

Servings:2

Cooking Time: 30 Minutes

Ingredients:

- 4 cups cauliflower florets (about ½ small head)
- 2 medium carrots, peeled, halved, and then sliced into quarters lengthwise
- 2 tablespoons olive oil, divided
- ½ teaspoon garlic powder, divided
- ½ teaspoon salt, divided
- 2 teaspoons za'atar spice mix, divided
- 1 can chickpeas, drained, rinsed, and patted dry
- ¾ cup plain Greek yogurt
- 1 teaspoon harissa spice paste

Directions:

1. Preheat the oven to 400ºF. Line a sheet pan with foil or parchment paper.

2. Place the cauliflower and carrots in a large bowl. Drizzle with 1 tablespoon olive oil and sprinkle with ¼ teaspoon of garlic powder, ¼ teaspoon of salt, and 1 teaspoon of za'atar. Toss well to combine.

3. Spread the vegetables onto one half of the sheet pan in a single layer.

4. Place the chickpeas in the same bowl and season with the remaining 1 tablespoon of oil, ¼ teaspoon of garlic powder, and ¼ teaspoon of salt, and the remaining za'atar. Toss well to combine.

5. Spread the chickpeas onto the other half of the sheet pan.

6. Roast for 30 minutes, or until the vegetables are tender and the chickpeas start to turn golden. Flip the vegetables halfway through the cooking time, and give the chickpeas a stir so they cook evenly.

7. The chickpeas may need an extra few minutes if you like them crispy. If so, remove the vegetables and leave the chickpeas in until they're cooked to desired crispiness.

8. Meanwhile, combine the yogurt and harissa in a small bowl. Taste and add additional harissa as desired, then serve.

Nutrition Info:

- Info Per Serving: Calories: 468;Fat: 23.0g;Protein: 18.1g;Carbs: 54.1g.

Simple Braised Carrots

Servings:4

Cooking Time:20 Minutes

Ingredients:

- 2 tbsp butter
- 1 lb carrots, cut into sticks
- ¾ cup water
- ¼ cup orange juice
- 1 tbsp honey
- Salt and white pepper to taste
- 1 tsp rosemary leaves

Directions:

1. Combine all the ingredients, except for the carrots and rosemary, in a heavy saucepan over medium heat and bring to a boil. Add carrots and cover. Turn the heat to a simmer and continue to cook for 5–8 minutes until carrots are soft when pierced with a knife. Remove the carrots to a serving plate. Then, increase heat to high and bring the liquid to a boil. Boil until the liquid has reduced and syrupy, about 4 minutes. Drizzle the sauce over the carrots and sprinkle with rosemary. Serve warm.

Nutrition Info:

- Info Per Serving: Calories: 122;Fat: 6g;Protein: 1g;Carbs: 17g.

Baked Veggie Medley

Servings:4
Cooking Time:70 Minutes
Ingredients:

- 2 tbsp olive oil
- ½ lb green beans, trimmed
- 1 tomato, chopped
- 1 potato, sliced
- ½ tbsp tomato paste
- 2 tbsp chopped fresh parsley
- 1 tsp sweet paprika
- 1 onion, sliced
- 1 cup mushrooms, sliced
- 1 celery stalk, chopped
- 1 red bell pepper, sliced
- 1 eggplant, sliced
- ½ cup vegetable broth
- Salt and black pepper to taste

Directions:

1. Preheat oven to 375 F. Warm oil in a skillet over medium heat and sauté onion, bell pepper, celery, and mushrooms for 5 minutes until tender. Stir in paprika and tomato paste for 1 minute. Pour in the vegetable broth and stir. Combine the remaining ingredients in a baking pan and mix in the sautéed vegetable. Bake covered with foil for 40-50 minutes.

Nutrition Info:

- Info Per Serving: Calories: 175;Fat: 8g;Protein: 5.2g;Carbs: 25.2g.

Mini Crustless Spinach Quiches

Servings:6
Cooking Time: 20 Minutes
Ingredients:

- 2 tablespoons extra-virgin olive oil
- 1 onion, finely chopped
- 2 cups baby spinach
- 2 garlic cloves, minced
- 8 large eggs, beaten
- ¼ cup unsweetened almond milk
- ½ teaspoon sea salt
- ¼ teaspoon freshly ground black pepper
- 1 cup shredded Swiss cheese
- Cooking spray

Directions:

1. Preheat the oven to 375ºF. Spritz a 6-cup muffin tin with cooking spray. Set aside.
2. In a large skillet over medium-high heat, heat the olive oil until shimmering. Add the onion and cook for about 4 minutes, or until soft. Add the spinach and cook for about 1 minute, stirring constantly, or until the spinach softens. Add the garlic and sauté for 30 seconds. Remove from the heat and let cool.
3. In a medium bowl, whisk together the eggs, milk, salt and pepper.
4. Stir the cooled vegetables and the cheese into the egg mixture. Spoon the mixture into the prepared muffin tins. Bake for about 15 minutes, or until the eggs are set.
5. Let rest for 5 minutes before serving.

Nutrition Info:

- Info Per Serving: Calories: 218;Fat: 17.0g;Protein: 14.0g;Carbs: 4.0g.

Baby Kale And Cabbage Salad

Servings:6
Cooking Time: 0 Minutes
Ingredients:

- 2 bunches baby kale, thinly sliced
- ½ head green savoy cabbage, cored and thinly sliced
- 1 medium red bell pepper, thinly sliced
- 1 garlic clove, thinly sliced
- 1 cup toasted peanuts
- Dressing:
- Juice of 1 lemon
- ¼ cup apple cider vinegar
- 1 teaspoon ground cumin
- ¼ teaspoon smoked paprika

Directions:

1. In a large mixing bowl, toss together the kale and cabbage.
2. Make the dressing: Whisk together the lemon juice, vinegar, cumin and paprika in a small bowl.
3. Pour the dressing over the greens and gently massage with your hands.
4. Add the pepper, garlic and peanuts to the mixing bowl. Toss to combine.
5. Serve immediately.

Nutrition Info:

- Info Per Serving: Calories: 199;Fat: 12.0g;Protein: 10.0g;Carbs: 17.0g.

Fish & Chickpea Stew

Servings:4
Cooking Time:30 Minutes
Ingredients:

- 3 tbsp olive oil
- 1 lb tilapia fish, cubed
- 1 lb canned chickpeas
- 1 cup canned tomatoes
- 1 parsnip, chopped
- 1 bell pepper, chopped
- ½ cup shallots, chopped
- 1 tsp garlic puree
- ½ tsp dried basil
- 1 bay leaf
- ¼ cup dry white wine
- 1 cup fish stock
- 2 cups vegetable broth
- Salt and black pepper to taste

Directions:

1. Warm the oil in a pot over medium heat. Add in parsnip, bell pepper, garlic, and shallots and cook for 3-5 minutes. Add in basil and bay leaf. Cook for another 30-40 seconds. Pour in white wine to scrape off any bits from the bottom.
2. Stir in fish stock, vegetable broth, and tomatoes. Bring to a boil, lower the heat, and simmer for 10 minutes. Mix in fish, chickpeas, salt, and black pepper. Simmer covered for 10 minutes more. Adjust the taste and discard the bay leaf.

Nutrition Info:

- Info Per Serving: Calories: 469;Fat: 13g;Protein: 34g;Carbs: 55g.

Buttery Garlic Green Beans

Servings:6
Cooking Time:25 Minutes
Ingredients:

- 2 tbsp butter
- 1 lb green beans, trimmed
- 4 cups water
- 6 garlic cloves, minced
- 1 shallot, chopped
- Celery salt to taste
- ½ tsp red pepper flakes

Directions:

1. Pour 4 cups of water in a pot over high heat and bring to a boil. Cut the green beans in half crosswise. Reduce the heat and add in the green beans. Simmer for 6-8 minutes until crisp-tender but still vibrant green. Drain beans and set aside.
2. Melt the butter in a pan over medium heat and sauté garlic and shallot for 3 minutes until the garlic is slightly browned and fragrant. Stir in the beans and season with celery salt. Cook for 2–3 minutes. Serve topped with red pepper flakes.

Nutrition Info:

- Info Per Serving: Calories: 65;Fat: 4g;Protein: 2g;Carbs: 7g.

Creamy Polenta With Mushrooms

Servings:2
Cooking Time: 30 Minutes
Ingredients:

- ½ ounce dried porcini mushrooms (optional but recommended)
- 2 tablespoons olive oil
- 1 pound baby bella (cremini) mushrooms, quartered
- 1 large shallot, minced
- 1 garlic clove, minced
- 1 tablespoon flour
- 2 teaspoons tomato paste
- ½ cup red wine
- 1 cup mushroom stock (or reserved liquid from soaking the porcini mushrooms, if using)
- ½ teaspoon dried thyme
- 1 fresh rosemary sprig
- 1½ cups water
- ½ teaspoon salt
- ⅓ cup instant polenta
- 2 tablespoons grated Parmesan cheese

Directions:

1. If using the dried porcini mushrooms, soak them in 1 cup of hot water for about 15 minutes to soften them. When they're softened, scoop them out of the water, reserving the soaking liquid. Mince the porcini mushrooms.
2. Heat the olive oil in a large sauté pan over medium-high heat. Add the mushrooms, shallot, and garlic, and sauté for 10 minutes, or until the vegetables are wilted and starting to caramelize.
3. Add the flour and tomato paste, and cook for another 30 seconds. Add the red wine, mushroom stock or porcini soaking liquid, thyme, and rosemary. Bring the mixture to a boil, stirring constantly until it thickens. Reduce the heat and let it simmer for 10 minutes.
4. Meanwhile, bring the water to a boil in a saucepan and add salt.
5. Add the instant polenta and stir quickly while it thickens. Stir in the Parmesan cheese. Taste and add additional salt, if needed. Serve warm.

Nutrition Info:

- Info Per Serving: Calories: 450;Fat: 16.0g;Protein: 14.1g;Carbs: 57.8g.

Roasted Veggies And Brown Rice Bowl

Servings:4
Cooking Time: 20 Minutes
Ingredients:

- 2 cups cauliflower florets
- 2 cups broccoli florets
- 1 can chickpeas, drained and rinsed
- 1 cup carrot slices
- 2 to 3 tablespoons extra-virgin olive oil, divided
- Salt and freshly ground black pepper, to taste
- Nonstick cooking spray
- 2 cups cooked brown rice
- 2 to 3 tablespoons sesame seeds, for garnish
- Dressing:
- 3 to 4 tablespoons tahini
- 2 tablespoons honey
- 1 lemon, juiced
- 1 garlic clove, minced
- Salt and freshly ground black pepper, to taste

Directions:

1. Preheat the oven to 400ºF. Spritz two baking sheets with nonstick cooking spray.
2. Spread the cauliflower and broccoli on the first baking sheet and the second with the chickpeas and carrot slices.
3. Drizzle each sheet with half of the olive oil and sprinkle with salt and pepper. Toss to coat well.
4. Roast the chickpeas and carrot slices in the preheated oven for 10 minutes, leaving the carrots tender but crisp, and the cauliflower and broccoli for 20 minutes until fork-tender. Stir them once halfway through the cooking time.
5. Meanwhile, make the dressing: Whisk together the tahini, honey, lemon juice, garlic, salt, and pepper in a small bowl.
6. Divide the cooked brown rice among four bowls. Top each bowl evenly with roasted vegetables and dressing. Sprinkle the sesame seeds on top for garnish before serving.

Nutrition Info:

- Info Per Serving: Calories: 453;Fat: 17.8g;Protein: 12.1g;Carbs: 61.8g.

Parsley & Olive Zucchini Bake

Servings:6
Cooking Time:1 Hour 40 Minutes
Ingredients:

- 3 tbsp olive oil
- 1 can tomatoes, diced
- 2 lb zucchinis, sliced
- 1 onion, chopped
- Salt and black pepper to taste
- 3 garlic cloves, minced
- ¼ tsp dried oregano
- ¼ tsp red pepper flakes
- 10 Kalamata olives, chopped
- 2 tbsp fresh parsley, chopped

Directions:

1. Preheat oven to 325 F. Warm the olive oil in a saucepan over medium heat. Sauté zucchini for about 3 minutes per side; transfer to a bowl. Stir-fry the onion and salt in the same saucepan for 3-5 minutes, stirring occasionally until onion soft and lightly golden. Stir in garlic, oregano, and pepper flakes and cook until fragrant, about 30 seconds.
2. Add in olives, tomatoes, salt, and pepper, bring to a simmer, and cook for about 10 minutes, stirring occasionally. Return the zucchini, cover, and transfer the pot to the oven. Bake for 10-15 minutes. Sprinkle with parsley and serve.

Nutrition Info:

- Info Per Serving: Calories: 164;Fat: 6g;Protein: 1.5g;Carbs: 7.7g.

Stuffed Portobello Mushrooms With Spinach

Servings:4

Cooking Time: 20 Minutes

Ingredients:

- 8 large portobello mushrooms, stems removed
- 3 teaspoons extra-virgin olive oil, divided
- 1 medium red bell pepper, diced
- 4 cups fresh spinach
- ¼ cup crumbled feta cheese

Directions:

1. Preheat the oven to 450ºF.
2. Using a spoon to scoop out the gills of the mushrooms and discard them. Brush the mushrooms with 2 teaspoons of olive oil.
3. Arrange the mushrooms (cap-side down) on a baking sheet. Roast in the preheated oven for 20 minutes.
4. Meantime, in a medium skillet, heat the remaining olive oil over medium heat until it shimmers.
5. Add the bell pepper and spinach and sauté for 8 to 10 minutes, stirring occasionally, or until the spinach is wilted.
6. Remove the mushrooms from the oven to a paper towel-lined plate. Using a spoon to stuff each mushroom with the bell pepper and spinach mixture. Scatter the feta cheese all over.
7. Serve immediately.

Nutrition Info:

- Info Per Serving: Calories: 115;Fat: 5.9g;Protein: 7.2g;Carbs: 11.5g.

Sides , Salads, And Soups Recipes

Spinach & Bean Salad With Goat Cheese

Servings:4
Cooking Time:35 Minutes
Ingredients:

- 4 tbsp olive oil
- 1 garlic clove, minced
- ½ tsp cumin
- ½ tsp chili flakes
- 2 tbsp red wine vinegar
- 1 tbsp fresh lemon juice
- 1 tbsp fresh dill
- Salt to taste
- 1 can black beans
- 2 cups fresh baby spinach
- ¼ lb goat cheese, crumbled
- ½ cup spring onions, sliced
- 1 jalapeño pepper, chopped
- 2 bell peppers, chopped

Directions:

1. In a small bowl, combine the garlic, cumin, chili flakes, olive oil, vinegar, lemon juice, dill, and salt. Put in the fridge.
2. Mix the black beans, baby spinach, spring onions, jalapeño pepper, and bell pepper in another bowl. Remove the dressing from the fridge and pour over the salad; toss to coat. Top with the goat cheese and serve.

Nutrition Info:

- Info Per Serving: Calories: 633;Fat: 25g;Protein: 32g;Carbs: 72g.

Roasted Pepper & Tomato Soup

Servings:4
Cooking Time:30 Minutes
Ingredients:

- 1 cup roasted bell peppers, chopped
- 2 tbsp olive oil
- 3 tomatoes, cored and halved
- 2 cloves garlic, minced
- 1 yellow onion, quartered
- 1 celery stalk, chopped
- 1 carrot, shredded
- ½ tsp ground cumin
- ½ tsp chili pepper
- 4 cups vegetable broth
- ½ tsp red pepper flakes
- 2 tbsp fresh basil, chopped
- Salt and black pepper to taste
- ¼ cup crème fraîche

Directions:

1. Heat oven to 380 F. Arrange the tomatoes and peppers on a roasting pan. Drizzle olive oil over the vegetables. Roast for 20 minutes until charred. Remove, let cool, and peel them.
2. Heat olive oil in a pot over medium heat and sauté onion, garlic, celery, and carrots for 3-5 minutes until tender. Stir in chili pepper and cumin for 1-2 minutes.
3. Pour in roasted bell peppers and tomatoes, stir, then add in the vegetable broth. Season with salt and pepper. Bring to a boil and reduce the heat; simmer for 10 minutes. Using an immersion blender, purée the soup until smooth. Sprinkle with pepper flakes and basil. Serve topped with crème fraîche.

Nutrition Info:

- Info Per Serving: Calories: 164;Fat: 12g;Protein: 6.5g;Carbs: 9.8g.

Black Olive & Radish Salad

Servings:4
Cooking Time:10 Minutes
Ingredients:

- 2 tbsp olive oil
- 1 Romaine lettuce, shredded
- 1 lb red radishes, sliced
- 1 tbsp lemon zest
- Salt and black pepper to taste
- 2 tbsp parsley, chopped
- 1 small red onion, sliced
- 10 black olives, sliced

Directions:

1. Mix lemon zest, salt, pepper, parsley, olive oil, radishes, onion, olives, and lettuce in a bowl. Serve right away.

Nutrition Info:

- Info Per Serving: Calories: 80;Fat: 5g;Protein: 3g;Carbs: 4g.

Cannellini Bean Stew With Spinach

Servings:4
Cooking Time:45 Minutes
Ingredients:

- 2 tbsp olive oil
- 1 onion, chopped
- 2 cloves garlic, minced
- 2 carrots, peeled and chopped
- 1 cup celery, chopped
- 4 cups vegetable broth
- 1 cup cannellini beans, soaked
- 1 tsp dried thyme
- 1 tsp dried rosemary
- 1 bay leaf
- 1 cup spinach, torn
- Salt and black pepper to taste

Directions:

1. Preheat your Instant Pot on Sauté mode and warm olive oil. Stir in garlic and onion, and cook for 3 minutes until tender and fragrant. Mix in celery and carrots and cook for 2 to 3 minutes more until they start to soften. Add broth, bay leaf, thyme, rosemary, cannellini beans, and salt. Seal the lid and cook for 30 minutes on High Pressure. Do a quick pressure release. Stir in spinach and allow to sit for 2-4 minutes until the spinach wilts, and season with pepper and salt.

Nutrition Info:

- Info Per Serving: Calories: 285;Fat: 8.7g;Protein: 17g;Carbs: 36g.

Lebanese Crunchy Salad With Seeds

Servings:4

Cooking Time:15 Minutes

Ingredients:

- For the Salad
- 1 head Romaine lettuce, separated into leaves
- 1 cup sunflower seeds, toasted
- 1 Lebanese cucumber, sliced
- 1 tbsp cilantro, chopped
- 2 tbsp black olives, pitted
- 8 cherry tomatoes, halved
- For Dressing
- 1 lemon, juiced
- ½ tsp Mediterranean herb mix
- 2 tbsp onions, chopped
- ½ tsp paprika
- ½ tsp garlic, chopped
- Salt and black pepper to taste

Directions:

1. Toss all of the salad ingredients in a bowl. Whisk all of the dressing ingredients until creamy and smooth. Dress your salad and serve.

Nutrition Info:

- Info Per Serving: Calories: 210;Fat: 16g;Protein: 8g;Carbs: 7g.

Easy Spring Salad

Servings:4

Cooking Time:5 Minutes

Ingredients:

- 2 tbsp olive oil
- 2 tomatoes, cut into wedges
- 2 red bell peppers, chopped
- 1 cucumber, chopped
- 1 red onion, sliced
- 8 Kalamata olives, sliced
- ½ cup feta cheese, crumbled
- ¼ cup lime juice
- Salt and black pepper to taste

Directions:

1. Mix tomatoes, bell peppers, cucumber, onion, olives, lime juice, olive oil, salt, and pepper in a bowl. Divide between individual bowls and top with feta cheese to serve.

Nutrition Info:

- Info Per Serving: Calories: 330;Fat: 12g;Protein: 7g;Carbs: 17g.

Orange-honey Glazed Carrots

Servings:2
Cooking Time: 15 To 20 Minutes
Ingredients:

- ½ pound rainbow carrots, peeled
- 2 tablespoons fresh orange juice
- 1 tablespoon honey
- ½ teaspoon coriander
- Pinch salt

Directions:

1. Preheat the oven to 400ºF.
2. Cut the carrots lengthwise into slices of even thickness and place in a large bowl.
3. Stir together the orange juice, honey, coriander, and salt in a small bowl. Pour the orange juice mixture over the carrots and toss until well coated.
4. Spread the carrots in a baking dish in a single layer. Roast for 15 to 20 minutes until fork-tender.
5. Let cool for 5 minutes before serving.

Nutrition Info:

- Info Per Serving: Calories: 85;Fat: 0g;Protein: 1.0g;Carbs: 21.0g.

Lemony Lamb Stew

Servings:4
Cooking Time:60 Minutes
Ingredients:

- 2 potatoes, peeled, cut into bite-sized pieces
- 2 tbsp olive oil
- 1 onion, chopped
- 1 lb lamb neck, boneless
- 2 large carrots, chopped
- 1 tomato, diced
- 1 red bell pepper, chopped
- 2 garlic cloves, minced
- 2 tbsp parsley, chopped
- ¼ cup lemon juice
- Salt and black pepper to taste

Directions:

1. Warm the olive oil in your Instant Pot on Sauté. Add the meat and brown for 4-6 minutes, stirring occasionally. Stir in onion, carrot, and garlic and cook for 3 more minutes until softened. Pour in the tomato and 2 cups of water. Season with salt and pepper. Seal the lid and cook on High Pressure for 45 minutes. When ready, do a quick pressure release. Sprinkle with parsley. Serve into bowls and enjoy!

Nutrition Info:

- Info Per Serving: Calories: 251;Fat: 9.7g;Protein: 5g;Carbs: 34.2g.

Three-bean Salad With Black Olives

Servings:6

Cooking Time:15 Minutes

Ingredients:

- 1 lb green beans, trimmed
- 1 red onion, thinly sliced
- 2 tbsp marjoram, chopped
- ¼ cup black olives, chopped
- ½ cup canned cannellini beans
- ½ cup canned chickpeas
- 2 tbsp extra-virgin olive oil
- ½ cup balsamic vinegar
- ½ tsp dried oregano
- Salt and black pepper to taste

Directions:

1. Steam the green beans for about 2 minutes or until just tender. Drain and place them in an ice-water bath. Drain thoroughly and pat them dry with paper towels. Put them in a large bowl and toss with the remaining ingredients. Serve.

Nutrition Info:

- Info Per Serving: Calories: 187;Fat: 6g;Protein: 7g;Carbs: 27g.

Greens, Fennel, And Pear Soup With Cashews

Servings:4

Cooking Time: 15 Minutes

Ingredients:

- 2 tablespoons olive oil
- 1 fennel bulb, cut into ¼-inch-thick slices
- 2 leeks, white part only, sliced
- 2 pears, peeled, cored, and cut into ½-inch cubes
- 1 teaspoon sea salt
- ¼ teaspoon freshly ground black pepper
- ½ cup cashews
- 2 cups packed blanched spinach
- 3 cups low-sodium vegetable soup

Directions:

1. Heat the olive oil in a stockpot over high heat until shimmering.
2. Add the fennel and leeks, then sauté for 5 minutes or until tender.
3. Add the pears and sprinkle with salt and pepper, then sauté for another 3 minutes or until the pears are soft.
4. Add the cashews, spinach, and vegetable soup. Bring to a boil. Reduce the heat to low. Cover and simmer for 5 minutes.
5. Pour the soup in a food processor, then pulse until creamy and smooth.
6. Pour the soup back to the pot and heat over low heat until heated through.
7. Transfer the soup to a large serving bowl and serve immediately.

Nutrition Info:

- Info Per Serving: Calories: 266;Fat: 15.1g;Protein: 5.2g;Carbs: 32.9g.

Olive Tapenade Flatbread With Cheese

Servings:4

Cooking Time:35 Min + Chilling Time

Ingredients:

- For the flatbread
- 2 tbsp olive oil
- 2 ½ tsp dry yeast
- 1 ½ cups all-purpose flour
- ¾ tsp salt
- ½ cup lukewarm water
- ¼ tsp sugar
- For the tapenade
- 2 roasted red pepper slices, chopped
- ¼ cup extra-virgin olive oil
- 1 cup green olives, chopped
- 10 black olives, chopped
- 1 tbsp capers
- 1 garlic clove, minced
- 1 tbsp chopped basil leaves
- 1 tbsp chopped fresh oregano
- ¼ cup goat cheese, crumbled

Directions:

1. Combine lukewarm water, sugar, and yeast in a bowl. Set aside covered for 5 minutes. Mix the flour and salt in a bowl. Pour in the yeast mixture and mix. Knead until you obtain a ball. Place the dough onto a floured surface and knead for 5 minutes until soft. Leave the dough into an oiled bowl, covered to rise until it has doubled in size, about 40 minutes.

2. Preheat oven to 400 F. Cut the dough into 4 balls and roll each one out to a ½ inch thickness. Bake for 5 minutes. In a blender, mix black olives, roasted pepper, green olives, capers, garlic, oregano, basil, and olive oil for 20 seconds until coarsely chopped. Spread the olive tapenade on the flatbreads and top with goat cheese to serve.

Nutrition Info:

- Info Per Serving: Calories: 366;Fat: 19g;Protein: 7.3g;Carbs: 42g.

Tuscan-style Panzanella Salad

Servings:4

Cooking Time:25 Minutes

Ingredients:

- 2 cups mixed cherry tomatoes, quartered
- 4 bread slices, crusts removed, cubed
- 4 tbsp extra-virgin olive oil
- 1 cucumber, sliced
- ½ red onion, thinly sliced
- ¼ cup chopped fresh basil
- ½ tsp dried oregano
- 1 tbsp capers
- 1 garlic clove, minced
- ¼ cup red wine vinegar
- 2 anchovy fillets, chopped
- Salt and black pepper to taste

Directions:

1. Preheat oven to 320 F. Pour the bread cubes into a baking dish and drizzle with 2 tbsp of olive oil. Bake for 6-8 minutes, shaking occasionally until browned and crisp. Let cool. Toss the cooled bread, cherry tomatoes, cucumber, red onion, basil, anchovies, and capers in a serving dish.

2. In another bowl, whisk the remaining olive oil, oregano, red wine vinegar, and garlic. Adjust the seasoning with salt and pepper. Drizzle the dressing over the salad and toss to coat.

Nutrition Info:

- Info Per Serving: Calories: 228;Fat: 21.6g;Protein: 2g;Carbs: 8.2g.

Rich Chicken And Small Pasta Broth

Servings:6

Cooking Time: 4 Hours

Ingredients:

- 6 boneless, skinless chicken thighs
- 4 stalks celery, cut into ½-inch pieces
- 4 carrots, cut into 1-inch pieces
- 1 medium yellow onion, halved
- 2 garlic cloves, minced
- 2 bay leaves
- Sea salt and freshly ground black pepper, to taste
- 6 cups low-sodium chicken stock
- ½ cup stelline pasta
- ¼ cup chopped fresh flat-leaf parsley

Directions:

1. Combine the chicken thighs, celery, carrots, onion, and garlic in the slow cooker. Spread with bay leaves and sprinkle with salt and pepper. Toss to mix well.
2. Pour in the chicken stock. Put the lid on and cook on high for 4 hours or until the internal temperature of chicken reaches at least 165°F.
3. In the last 20 minutes of the cooking, remove the chicken from the slow cooker and transfer to a bowl to cool until ready to reserve.
4. Discard the bay leaves and add the pasta to the slow cooker. Put the lid on and cook for 15 minutes or until al dente.
5. Meanwhile, slice the chicken, then put the chicken and parsley in the slow cooker and cook for 5 minutes or until well combined.
6. Pour the soup in a large bowl and serve immediately.

Nutrition Info:

- Info Per Serving: Calories: 285;Fat: 10.8g;Protein: 27.4g;Carbs: 18.8g.

Cucumber Gazpacho

Servings:4

Cooking Time: 0 Minutes

Ingredients:

- 2 cucumbers, peeled, deseeded, and cut into chunks
- ½ cup mint, finely chopped
- 2 cups plain Greek yogurt
- 2 garlic cloves, minced
- 2 cups low-sodium vegetable soup
- 1 tablespoon no-salt-added tomato paste
- 3 teaspoons fresh dill
- Sea salt and freshly ground pepper, to taste

Directions:

1. Put the cucumber, mint, yogurt, and garlic in a food processor, then pulse until creamy and smooth.
2. Transfer the puréed mixture in a large serving bowl, then add the vegetable soup, tomato paste, dill, salt, and ground black pepper. Stir to mix well.
3. Keep the soup in the refrigerator for at least 2 hours, then serve chilled.

Nutrition Info:

- Info Per Serving: Calories: 133;Fat: 1.5g;Protein: 14.2g;Carbs: 16.5g.

Moroccan Spiced Couscous

Servings:2
Cooking Time: 8 Minutes
Ingredients:

- 1 tablespoon olive oil
- ¾ cup couscous
- ¼ teaspoon cinnamon
- ¼ teaspoon garlic powder
- ¼ teaspoon salt, plus more as needed
- 1 cup water
- 2 tablespoons minced dried apricots
- 2 tablespoons raisins
- 2 teaspoons minced fresh parsley

Directions:

1. Heat the olive oil in a saucepan over medium-high heat until it shimmers.
2. Add the couscous, cinnamon, garlic powder, and salt. Stir for 1 minute to toast the couscous and spices.
3. Add the water, apricots, and raisins and bring the mixture to a boil.
4. Cover and turn off the heat. Allow the couscous to sit for 4 to 5 minutes and then fluff it with a fork. Sprinkle with the fresh parsley. Season with more salt as needed and serve.

Nutrition Info:

- Info Per Serving: Calories: 338;Fat: 8.0g;Protein: 9.0g;Carbs: 59.0g.

Pork Chop & Arugula Salad

Servings:4
Cooking Time:50 Minutes
Ingredients:

- 1 lb pork chops
- 2 cups goat cheese, crumbled
- 2 garlic cloves, minced
- 2 tsp lemon zest
- ½ tsp thyme, chopped
- 2 cups arugula
- 1 tbsp lemon juice

Directions:

1. Preheat the oven to 390 F. Rub the pork chops with garlic, lemon zest, thyme, and lemon juice and arrange them on a greased baking pan. Roast for 30 minutes. Sprinkle with goat cheese and bake for another 10 minutes. Place the arugula on a platter and top with the pork chops to serve.

Nutrition Info:

- Info Per Serving: Calories: 670;Fat: 56g;Protein: 44g;Carbs: 5g.

Zesty Spanish Potato Salad

Servings:6
Cooking Time: 5 To 7 Minutes
Ingredients:

- 4 russet potatoes, peeled and chopped
- 3 large hard-boiled eggs, chopped
- 1 cup frozen mixed vegetables, thawed
- ½ cup plain, unsweetened, full-fat Greek yogurt
- 5 tablespoons pitted Spanish olives
- ½ teaspoon freshly ground black pepper
- ½ teaspoon dried mustard seed
- ½ tablespoon freshly squeezed lemon juice
- ½ teaspoon dried dill
- Salt, to taste

Directions:

1. Place the potatoes in a large pot of water and boil for 5 to 7 minutes, until just fork-tender, checking periodically for doneness. You don't have to overcook them.
2. Meanwhile, in a large bowl, mix the eggs, vegetables, yogurt, olives, pepper, mustard, lemon juice, and dill. Season with salt to taste. Once the potatoes are cooled somewhat, add them to the large bowl, then toss well and serve.

Nutrition Info:

- Info Per Serving: Calories: 192;Fat: 5.0g;Protein: 9.0g;Carbs: 30.0g.

Asparagus & Red Onion Side Dish

Servings:6
Cooking Time:20 Minutes
Ingredients:
- 2 tbsp olive oil
- 1 ½ lb asparagus spears
- 1 tsp garlic powder
- 1 red onion, sliced
- Salt and black pepper to taste

Directions:
1. Preheat oven to 390 F. Brush the asparagus with olive oil. Toss with garlic powder, salt, and black pepper. Roast in the oven for about 15 minutes. Top the roasted asparagus with the red onion. Serve and enjoy!

Nutrition Info:
- Info Per Serving: Calories: 129;Fat: 3g;Protein: 3g;Carbs: 7g.

Mackerel & Radish Salad

Servings:4
Cooking Time:5 Minutes
Ingredients:
- 3 tbsp olive oil
- 4 oz smoked mackerel, flaked
- 10 radishes, sliced
- 5 oz baby arugula
- 1 cup corn
- 2 tbsp lemon juice
- Sea salt to taste
- 2 tbsp fresh parsley, chopped

Directions:
1. Place the arugula on a serving plate. Top with corn, mackerel, and radishes.Mix olive oil, lemon juice, and salt in a bowl and pour the dressing over the salad. Top with parsley.

Nutrition Info:
- Info Per Serving: Calories: 300;Fat: 19g;Protein: 19g;Carbs: 23g.

Baby Spinach & Apple Salad With Walnuts

Servings:4
Cooking Time:5 Minutes
Ingredients:
- 2 oz sharp white cheddar cheese, cubed
- 3 tbsp olive oil
- 8 cups baby spinach
- 1 Granny Smith apple, diced
- 1 medium red apple, diced
- ½ cup toasted pecans
- 1 tbsp apple cider vinegar

Directions:
1. Toss the spinach, apples, pecans, and cubed cheese together. Lightly drizzle olive oil and vinegar over the top and serve.

Nutrition Info:
- Info Per Serving: Calories: 138;Fat: 12.8g;Protein: 1g;Carbs: 7g.

Cherry & Pine Nut Couscous

Servings:6
Cooking Time:10 Minutes
Ingredients:

- 2 tbsp olive oil
- 3 cups hot water
- 1 cup couscous
- ½ cup pine nuts, roasted
- ½ cup dry cherries, chopped
- ½ cup parsley, chopped
- Salt and black pepper to taste
- 1 tbsp lime juice

Directions:

1. Place couscous and hot water in a bowl and let sit for 10 minutes. Fluff with a fork and remove to a bowl. Stir in pine nuts, cherries, parsley, salt, pepper, lime juice, and olive oil.

Nutrition Info:

- Info Per Serving: Calories: 220;Fat: 8g;Protein: 6g;Carbs: 9g.

Garbanzo & Arugula Salad With Blue Cheese

Servings:4
Cooking Time:10 Minutes
Ingredients:

- 15 oz canned garbanzo beans, drained
- ½ cup Gorgonzola cheese, crumbled
- 3 tbsp olive oil
- 1 cucumber, cubed
- 3 oz black olives, sliced
- 1 Roma tomato, slivered
- ¼ cup red onion, chopped
- 5 cups arugula
- Salt to taste
- 1 tbsp lemon juice
- 2 tbsp parsley, chopped

Directions:

1. Place the arugula in a salad bowl. Add in garbanzo beans, cucumber, olives, tomato, and onion and mix to combine. In another small bowl, whisk the lemon juice, olive oil, and salt. Drizzle the dressing over the salad and sprinkle with gorgonzola cheese and parsley to serve.

Nutrition Info:

- Info Per Serving: Calories: 280;Fat: 17g;Protein: 10g;Carbs: 25g.

Octopus, Calamari & Watercress Salad

Servings:4
Cooking Time:50 Minutes
Ingredients:

- 2 tbsp olive oil
- 2 cups olives, sliced
- 1 octopus, tentacles separated
- 2 oz calamari rings
- 3 garlic cloves, minced
- 1 white onion, chopped
- ¾ cup chicken stock
- 2 cups watercress, sliced
- 1 cup parsley, chopped
- Salt and black pepper to taste
- 1 tbsp red wine vinegar

Directions:

1. Place octopus, stock, calamari rings, salt, and pepper in a pot over medium heat and bring to a simmer. Cook for 40 minutes. Strain seafood and let cool completely. Chop tentacles into pieces. Remove to a serving bowl along with the calamari rings. Stir in garlic, onion, watercress, olives, parsley, red wine vinegar, and olive oil and toss to coat.

Nutrition Info:

- Info Per Serving: Calories: 300;Fat: 11g;Protein: 9g;Carbs: 23g.

The Ultimate Chicken Bean Soup

Servings:6
Cooking Time:40 Minutes
Ingredients:

- 3 tbsp olive oil
- 3 garlic cloves, minced
- 1 onion, chopped
- 3 tomatoes, chopped
- 4 cups chicken stock
- 1 lb chicken breasts, cubed
- 1 red chili pepper, chopped
- 1 tbsp fennel seeds, crushed
- 14 oz canned white beans
- 1 lime, zested and juiced
- Salt and black pepper to taste
- 2 tbsp parsley, chopped

Directions:

1. Warm the olive oil in a pot over medium heat. Cook the onion and garlic, adding a splash of water, for 10 minutes until aromatic. Add in the chicken and chili pepper and sit-fry for another 6-8 minutes. Put in tomatoes, chicken stock, beans, lime zest, lime juice, salt, pepper, and fennel seeds and bring to a boil; cook for 30 minutes. Serve topped with parsley.

Nutrition Info:

- Info Per Serving: Calories: 670;Fat: 18g;Protein: 56g;Carbs: 74g.

Roasted Red Pepper & Olive Spread

Servings:6
Cooking Time:10 Minutes
Ingredients:

- ¼ tsp dried thyme
- 1 tbsp capers
- ½ cup pitted green olives
- 1 roasted red pepper, chopped
- 1 tsp balsamic vinegar
- 2/3 cup soft bread crumbs
- 2 cloves garlic, minced
- ½ tsp red pepper flakes
- 1/3 cup extra-virgin olive oil

Directions:

1. Place all the ingredients, except for the olive oil, in a food processor and blend until chunky. With the machine running, slowly pour in the olive oil until it is well combined. Refrigerate or serve at room temperature.

Nutrition Info:

- Info Per Serving: Calories: 467;Fat: 38g;Protein: 5g;Carbs: 27g.

Citrus Salad With Kale And Fennel

Servings:2
Cooking Time: 0 Minutes

Ingredients:

- Dressing:
- 3 tablespoons olive oil
- 2 tablespoons fresh orange juice
- 1 tablespoon blood orange vinegar, other orange vinegar, or cider vinegar
- 1 tablespoon honey
- Salt and freshly ground black pepper, to taste
- Salad:
- 2 cups packed baby kale
- 1 medium navel or blood orange, segmented
- ½ small fennel bulb, stems and leaves removed, sliced into matchsticks
- 3 tablespoons toasted pecans, chopped
- 2 ounces goat cheese, crumbled

Directions:

1. Make the Dressing
2. Mix the olive oil, orange juice, vinegar, and honey in a small bowl and whisk to combine. Season with salt and pepper to taste. Set aside.
3. Make the Salad
4. Divide the baby kale, orange segments, fennel, pecans, and goat cheese evenly between two plates.
5. Drizzle half of the dressing over each salad, and serve.

Nutrition Info:

- Info Per Serving: Calories: 503;Fat: 39.1g;Protein: 13.2g;Carbs: 31.2g.

Beans , Grains, And Pastas Recipes

Moroccan-style Vegetable Bean Stew

Servings:6
Cooking Time:50 Minutes
Ingredients:

- 3 tbsp olive oil
- 1 onion, chopped
- 8 oz Swiss chard, torn
- 4 garlic cloves, minced
- 1 tsp ground cumin
- ½ tsp paprika
- ½ tsp ground coriander
- ¼ tsp ground cinnamon
- 2 tbsp tomato paste
- 2 tbsp cornstarch
- 4 cups vegetable broth
- 2 carrots, chopped
- 1 can chickpeas
- 1 can butter beans
- 3 tbsp minced fresh parsley
- 3 tbsp harissa sauce
- Salt and black pepper to taste

Directions:

1. Warm the olive oil in a saucepan over medium heat. Sauté the onion until softened, about 3 minutes. Stir in garlic, cumin, paprika, coriander, and cinnamon and cook until fragrant, about 30 seconds. Stir in tomato paste and cornstarch and cook for 1 minute. Pour in broth and carrots, scraping up any browned bits, smoothing out any lumps, and bringing to boil. Reduce to a gentle simmer and cook for 10 minutes. Stir in chard, chickpeas, beans, salt, and pepper and simmer until vegetables are tender, 10-15 minutes. Sprinkle with parsley and some harissa sauce. Serve with the remaining sauce harissa on the side.

Nutrition Info:

- Info Per Serving: Calories: 387;Fat: 3.2g;Protein: 7g;Carbs: 28.7g.

Mint & Lemon Cranberry Beans

Servings:6
Cooking Time:1 Hour 45 Minutes
Ingredients:

- ¼ cup olive oil
- Salt and black pepper to taste
- 1 lb cranberry beans, soaked
- 1 onion, chopped
- 2 carrots, chopped
- 4 garlic cloves, sliced thin
- 1 tbsp tomato paste
- 2 tomatoes, chopped
- ½ tsp paprika
- ½ cup dry white wine
- 4 cups vegetable broth
- 2 tbsp lemon juice
- 2 tbsp minced fresh mint

Directions:

1. Preheat oven to 350 F. Warm the olive oil in a pot over medium heat. Sauté the onion and carrots until softened, about 5 minutes. Stir in garlic, tomato paste, tomatoes, paprika, salt, and pepper and cook until fragrant, about 1 minute. Stir in wine, scraping up any browned bits. Stir in broth, ½ cup of water, and beans and bring to boil. Place in the oven and cook covered for about 1 ½ hours, stirring every 30 minutes until the beans are tender. Sprinkle with lemon juice and mint. Serve.

Nutrition Info:

- Info Per Serving: Calories: 248;Fat: 8.6g;Protein: 3g;Carbs: 9.5g.

Parsley Beef Fusilli

Servings:4
Cooking Time:30 Minutes
Ingredients:

- 1 cup grated Pecorino Romano cheese
- 1 lb thick-cut New York strip steaks, cut into 1-inch cubes
- 4 tbsp butter
- 16 oz fusilli pasta
- Salt and black pepper to taste
- 4 garlic cloves, minced
- 2 tbsp chopped fresh parsley

Directions:

1. In a pot of boiling water, cook the fusilli pasta for 8-10 minutes until al dente. Drain and set aside.
2. Melt the butter in a large skillet, season the steaks with salt, black pepper and cook in the butter until brown, and cooked through, 10 minutes. Stir in the garlic and cook until fragrant, 1 minute. Mix in the parsley and fusilli pasta; toss well and season with salt and black pepper. Dish the food, top with the Pecorino Romano cheese and serve immediately.

Nutrition Info:

- Info Per Serving: Calories: 422;Fat: 22g;Protein: 36g;Carbs: 17g.

Israeli Couscous With Asparagus

Servings:6
Cooking Time: 25 Minutes
Ingredients:

- 1½ pounds asparagus spears, ends trimmed and stalks chopped into 1-inch pieces
- 1 garlic clove, minced
- 1 tablespoon extra-virgin olive oil
- ¼ teaspoon freshly ground black pepper
- 1¾ cups water
- 1 box uncooked whole-wheat or regular Israeli couscous
- ¼ teaspoon kosher salt
- 1 cup garlic-and-herb goat cheese, at room temperature

Directions:

1. Preheat the oven to 425°F.
2. In a large bowl, stir together the asparagus, garlic, oil, and pepper. Spread the asparagus on a large, rimmed baking sheet and roast for 10 minutes, stirring a few times. Remove the pan from the oven, and spoon the asparagus into a large serving bowl. Set aside.
3. While the asparagus is roasting, bring the water to a boil in a medium saucepan. Add the couscous and season with salt, stirring well.
4. Reduce the heat to medium-low. Cover and cook for 12 minutes, or until the water is absorbed.
5. Pour the hot couscous into the bowl with the asparagus. Add the goat cheese and mix thoroughly until completely melted.
6. Serve immediately.

Nutrition Info:

- Info Per Serving: Calories: 103;Fat: 2.0g;Protein: 6.0g;Carbs: 18.0g.

Rice And Blueberry Stuffed Sweet Potatoes

Servings:4
Cooking Time: 20 Minutes

Ingredients:

* 2 cups cooked wild rice
* ½ cup dried blueberries
* ½ cup chopped hazelnuts
* ½ cup shredded Swiss chard
* 1 teaspoon chopped fresh thyme
* 1 scallion, white and green parts, peeled and thinly sliced
* Sea salt and freshly ground black pepper, to taste
* 4 sweet potatoes, baked in the skin until tender

Directions:

1. Preheat the oven to 400ºF.
2. Combine all the ingredients, except for the sweet potatoes, in a large bowl. Stir to mix well.
3. Cut the top third of the sweet potato off length wire, then scoop most of the sweet potato flesh out.
4. Fill the potato with the wild rice mixture, then set the sweet potato on a greased baking sheet.
5. Bake in the preheated oven for 20 minutes or until the sweet potato skin is lightly charred.
6. Serve immediately.

Nutrition Info:

* Info Per Serving: Calories: 393;Fat: 7.1g;Protein: 10.2g;Carbs: 76.9g.

Oregano Chicken Risotto

Servings:4
Cooking Time:45 Minutes

Ingredients:

* 4 chicken thighs, bone-in and skin-on
* 2 tbsp olive oil
* 1 cup arborio rice
* 2 lemons, juiced
* 1 tsp oregano, dried
* 1 red onion, chopped
* Salt and black pepper to taste
* 2 garlic cloves, minced
* 2 ½ cups chicken stock
* 1 cup green olives, sliced
* 2 tbsp parsley, chopped
* ½ cup Parmesan, grated

Directions:

1. Warm the olive oil in a skillet over medium heat and brown chicken thighs skin-side down for 3-4 minutes, turn, and cook for 3 minutes. Remove to a plate. Place garlic and onion in the same skillet and sauté for 3 minutes. Stir in rice, salt, pepper, oregano, and lemon juice. Add 1 cup of chicken stock, reduce the heat and simmer the rice while stirring until it is absorbed. Add another cup of chicken broth and continue simmering until the stock is absorbed. Pour in the remaining chicken stock and return the chicken; cook until the rice is tender. Turn the heat off. Stir in Parmesan cheese and top with olives and parsley. Serve into plates. Enjoy!

Nutrition Info:

* Info Per Serving: Calories: 450;Fat: 19g;Protein: 26g;Carbs: 28g.

Raspberry & Nut Quinoa

Servings:4
Cooking Time:5 Minutes
Ingredients:

- 1 tbsp honey
- 2 cups almond milk
- 2 cups quinoa, cooked
- ½ tsp cinnamon powder
- 1 cup raspberries
- ¼ cup walnuts, chopped

Directions:
1. Combine quinoa, milk, cinnamon powder, honey, raspberries, and walnuts in a bowl. Serve in individual bowls.

Nutrition Info:

- Info Per Serving: Calories: 300;Fat: 15g;Protein: 5g;Carbs: 15g.

Greek-style Chickpea Salad

Servings:6
Cooking Time:15 Minutes
Ingredients:

- ¼ cup extra-virgin olive oil
- 2 cans chickpeas
- 1 cucumber, sliced
- 2 tbsp lemon juice
- Salt and black pepper to taste
- 2 tomatoes, chopped
- 1 cup baby arugula
- 12 Kalamata olives, chopped

Directions:
1. Whish the olive oil, lemon juice, salt, and pepperin a salad bowl. Add the tomatoes, cucumber, arugula, and olives and toss to combine. Serve immediately or refrigerate in an airtight glass container for up to 1 day.

Nutrition Info:

- Info Per Serving: Calories: 222;Fat: 12.7g;Protein: 6g;Carbs: 22g.

Lentil And Mushroom Pasta

Servings:2
Cooking Time: 50 Minutes
Ingredients:

- 2 tablespoons olive oil
- 1 large yellow onion, finely diced
- 2 portobello mushrooms, trimmed and chopped finely
- 2 tablespoons tomato paste
- 3 garlic cloves, chopped
- 1 teaspoon oregano
- 2½ cups water
- 1 cup brown lentils
- 1 can diced tomatoes with basil (with juice if diced)
- 1 tablespoon balsamic vinegar
- 8 ounces pasta of choice, cooked
- Salt and black pepper, to taste
- Chopped basil, for garnish

Directions:
1. Place a large stockpot over medium heat. Add the oil. Once the oil is hot, add the onion and mushrooms. Cover and cook until both are soft, about 5 minutes. Add the tomato paste, garlic, and oregano and cook 2 minutes, stirring constantly.
2. Stir in the water and lentils. Bring to a boil, then reduce the heat to medium-low and cook for 5 minutes, covered.
3. Add the tomatoes (and juice if using diced) and vinegar. Replace the lid, reduce the heat to low and cook until the lentils are tender, about 30 minutes.
4. Remove the sauce from the heat and season with salt and pepper to taste. Garnish with the basil and serve over the cooked pasta.

Nutrition Info:

- Info Per Serving: Calories: 463;Fat: 15.9g;Protein: 12.5g;Carbs: 70.8g.

Moroccan Rice Pilaf

Servings:4
Cooking Time:40 Minutes
Ingredients:

- 2 tbsp olive oil
- ¼ cup pine nuts
- 1 ¼ cups brown rice
- 1 onion, diced
- 2 cups chicken stock
- 1 cinnamon stick
- ¼ cup dried apricots, chopped
- Salt and black pepper to taste

Directions:

1. Warm the olive oil in a large saucepan over medium heat.
2. Sauté the onions and pine nuts for 5-7 minutes, or until the pine nuts are golden and the onion is translucent. Add the rice and sauté for 2 minutes until lightly browned. Pour the stock and bring it to a boil. Add the cinnamon and apricots.
3. Lower the heat, cover the pan, and simmer for 17-20 minutes or until the rice is tender and the liquid is mostly absorbed. When ready, remove from the heat and fluff with a fork. Season to taste and serve warm.

Nutrition Info:

- Info Per Serving: Calories: 510;Fat: 24g;Protein: 13g;Carbs: 62g.

Tomato Sauce And Basil Pesto Fettuccine

Servings:4
Cooking Time: 15 Minutes
Ingredients:

- 4 Roma tomatoes, diced
- 2 teaspoons no-salt-added tomato paste
- 1 tablespoon chopped fresh oregano
- 2 garlic cloves, minced
- 1 cup low-sodium vegetable soup
- ½ teaspoon sea salt
- 1 packed cup fresh basil leaves
- ¼ cup pine nuts
- ¼ cup grated Parmesan cheese
- 2 tablespoons extra-virgin olive oil
- 1 pound cooked whole-grain fettuccine

Directions:

1. Put the tomatoes, tomato paste, oregano, garlic, vegetable soup, and salt in a skillet. Stir to mix well.
2. Cook over medium heat for 10 minutes or until lightly thickened.
3. Put the remaining ingredients, except for the fettuccine, in a food processor and pulse to combine until smooth.
4. Pour the puréed basil mixture into the tomato mixture, then add the fettuccine. Cook for a few minutes or until heated through and the fettuccine is well coated.
5. Serve immediately.

Nutrition Info:

- Info Per Serving: Calories: 389;Fat: 22.7g;Protein: 9.7g;Carbs: 40.2g.

Tomato Bean & Sausage Casserole

Servings:4
Cooking Time:45 Minutes
Ingredients:

- 2 tbsp olive oil
- 1 lb Italian sausages
- 1 can cannellini beans
- 1 carrot, chopped
- 1 onion, chopped
- 2 garlic cloves, minced
- 1 tsp paprika
- 1 can tomatoes, diced
- 1 celery stalk, chopped
- Salt and black pepper to taste

Directions:

1. Preheat oven to 350 F. Warm olive oil in a pot over medium heat. Sauté onion, garlic, celery, and carrot for 3-4 minutes, stirring often until softened. Add in sausages and cook for another 3 minutes, turning occasionally. Stir in paprika for 30 seconds. Heat off. Mix in tomatoes, beans, salt, and pepper. Pour into a baking dish and bake for 30 minutes.

Nutrition Info:

- Info Per Serving: Calories: 862;Fat: 44g;Protein: 43g;Carbs: 76g.

Ziti Marinara Bake

Servings:4
Cooking Time:60 Minutes
Ingredients:

- For the Marinara Sauce:
- 2 tbsp olive oil
- ¼ onion, diced
- 3 cloves garlic, chopped
- 1 can tomatoes, diced
- Sprig of fresh thyme
- ½ bunch fresh basil
- Salt and pepper to taste
- For the Ziti:
- 1 lb ziti
- 3 ½ cups marinara sauce
- 1 cup cottage cheese
- 1 cup grated Mozzarella
- ¾ cup grated Pecorino cheese

Directions:

1. In a saucepan, warm the olive oil over medium heat. Stir-fry onion and garlic until lightly browned, 3 minutes. Add the tomatoes and herbs, and bring to a boil, then simmer for 7 minutes, covered. Set aside. Discard the herb sprigs and stir in sea salt and black pepper to taste.
2. Preheat the oven to 375F. Prepare the pasta according to package directions. Drain and mix the pasta in a bowl along with 2 cups of marinara sauce, cottage cheese, and half the Mozzarella and Pecorino cheeses. Transfer the mixture to a baking dish, and top with the remaining marinara sauce and cheese. Bake for 25 to 35 minutes, or until bubbly and golden brown. Serve warm.

Nutrition Info:

- Info Per Serving: Calories: 455;Fat: 17g;Protein: 19g;Carbs: 62g.

Wild Rice, Celery, And Cauliflower Pilaf

Servings:4
Cooking Time: 45 Minutes
Ingredients:

- 1 tablespoon olive oil, plus more for greasing the baking dish
- 1 cup wild rice
- 2 cups low-sodium chicken broth
- 1 sweet onion, chopped
- 2 stalks celery, chopped
- 1 teaspoon minced garlic
- 2 carrots, peeled, halved lengthwise, and sliced
- ½ cauliflower head, cut into small florets
- 1 teaspoon chopped fresh thyme
- Sea salt, to taste

Directions:

1. Preheat the oven to 350°F. Line a baking sheet with parchment paper and grease with olive oil.
2. Put the wild rice in a saucepan, then pour in the chicken broth. Bring to a boil. Reduce the heat to low and simmer for 30 minutes or until the rice is plump.
3. Meanwhile, heat the remaining olive oil in an oven-proof skillet over medium-high heat until shimmering.
4. Add the onion, celery, and garlic to the skillet and sauté for 3 minutes or until the onion is translucent.
5. Add the carrots and cauliflower to the skillet and sauté for 5 minutes. Turn off the heat and set aside.
6. Pour the cooked rice in the skillet with the vegetables. Sprinkle with thyme and salt.
7. Set the skillet in the preheated oven and bake for 15 minutes or until the vegetables are soft.
8. Serve immediately.

Nutrition Info:

- Info Per Serving: Calories: 214;Fat: 3.9g;Protein: 7.2g;Carbs: 37.9g.

Tomato Basil Pasta

Servings:2
Cooking Time: 2 Minutes
Ingredients:

- 2 cups dried campanelle or similar pasta
- 1¾ cups vegetable stock
- ½ teaspoon salt, plus more as needed
- 2 tomatoes, cut into large dices
- 1 or 2 pinches red pepper flakes
- ½ teaspoon garlic powder
- ½ teaspoon dried oregano
- 10 to 12 fresh sweet basil leaves
- Freshly ground black pepper, to taste

Directions:

1. In your Instant Pot, stir together the pasta, stock, and salt. Scatter the tomatoes on top (do not stir).
2. Secure the lid. Select the Manual mode and set the cooking time for 2 minutes at High Pressure.
3. Once cooking is complete, do a quick pressure release. Carefully open the lid.
4. Stir in the red pepper flakes, oregano, and garlic powder. If there's more than a few tablespoons of liquid in the bottom, select Sauté and cook for 2 to 3 minutes until it evaporates.
5. When ready to serve, chiffonade the basil and stir it in. Taste and season with more salt and pepper, as needed. Serve warm.

Nutrition Info:

- Info Per Serving: Calories: 415;Fat: 2.0g;Protein: 15.2g;Carbs: 84.2g.

Traditional Mushroom Risotto

Servings:6
Cooking Time:33 Minutes
Ingredients:

- ½ cup Pecorino-Romano cheese, grated
- 2 tbsp olive oil
- 2 oz dried porcini mushrooms
- 4 ½ cups chicken stock
- 1 onion, minced
- 2 cups brown rice
- Salt and black pepper to taste

Directions:

1. Cover the mushrooms in a bowl with hot water. Set aside for 25 minutes. Then drain them, keeping the liquid, and rinse. Strain the liquid through a sieve lined with cheesecloth. Add the liquid to the stock. Warm the stock and mushroom liquid in a saucepan until it simmers. Lower the heat.
2. Warm the olive oil in a saucepan over medium heat. Sauté onion for 5 minutes. Stir in the rice and mushrooms and ¾ cup of stock. Cook the rice, stirring constantly, adding more liquid, so the rice can absorb the liquid until it's tender, 20-30 minutes. Always keep some liquid visible in the pan. Remove from the heat, stir in the cheese, and season to taste.

Nutrition Info:

- Info Per Serving: Calories: 305;Fat: 8g;Protein: 8g;Carbs: 56g.

Cumin Quinoa Pilaf

Servings:2
Cooking Time: 5 Minutes
Ingredients:

- 2 tablespoons extra virgin olive oil
- 2 cloves garlic, minced
- 3 cups water
- 2 cups quinoa, rinsed
- 2 teaspoons ground cumin
- 2 teaspoons turmeric
- Salt, to taste
- 1 handful parsley, chopped

Directions:

1. Press the Sauté button to heat your Instant Pot.
2. Once hot, add the oil and garlic to the pot, stir and cook for 1 minute.
3. Add water, quinoa, cumin, turmeric, and salt, stirring well.
4. Lock the lid. Select the Manual mode and set the cooking time for 1 minute at High Pressure.
5. When the timer beeps, perform a natural pressure release for 10 minutes, then release any remaining pressure. Carefully remove the lid.
6. Fluff the quinoa with a fork. Season with more salt, if needed.
7. Sprinkle parsley on top and serve.

Nutrition Info:

- Info Per Serving: Calories: 384;Fat: 12.3g;Protein: 12.8g;Carbs: 57.4g.

Pearl Barley Risotto With Parmesan Cheese

Servings:6

Cooking Time: 20 Minutes

Ingredients:

- 4 cups low-sodium or no-salt-added vegetable broth
- 1 tablespoon extra-virgin olive oil
- 1 cup chopped yellow onion
- 2 cups uncooked pearl barley
- ½ cup dry white wine
- 1 cup freshly grated Parmesan cheese, divided
- ¼ teaspoon kosher or sea salt
- ¼ teaspoon freshly ground black pepper
- Fresh chopped chives and lemon wedges, for serving (optional)

Directions:

1. Pour the broth into a medium saucepan and bring to a simmer.
2. Heat the olive oil in a large stockpot over medium-high heat. Add the onion and cook for about 4 minutes, stirring occasionally.
3. Add the barley and cook for 2 minutes, stirring, or until the barley is toasted. Pour in the wine and cook for about 1 minute, or until most of the liquid evaporates. Add 1 cup of the warm broth into the pot and cook, stirring, for about 2 minutes, or until most of the liquid is absorbed.
4. Add the remaining broth, 1 cup at a time, cooking until each cup is absorbed before adding the next. The last addition of broth will take a bit longer to absorb, about 4 minutes.
5. Remove the pot from the heat, and stir in ½ cup of the cheese, and the salt and pepper.
6. Serve with the remaining ½ cup of the cheese on the side, along with the chives and lemon wedges (if desired).

Nutrition Info:

- Info Per Serving: Calories: 421;Fat: 11.0g;Protein: 15.0g;Carbs: 67.0g.

Authentic Fettuccine A La Puttanesca

Servings:4

Cooking Time:20 Minutes

Ingredients:

- 2 tbsp extra-virgin olive oil
- 20 Kalamata olives, chopped
- ¼ cup fresh basil, chopped
- 4 garlic cloves, minced
- 2 anchovy fillets, chopped
- ¼ tsp red pepper flakes
- 3 tbsp capers
- 3 cans diced tomatoes
- 8 oz fettuccine pasta
- 2 tbsp Parmesan cheese, grated
- Salt and black pepper to taste

Directions:

1. Cook the fettuccine pasta according to pack instructions, drain and let it to cool. Warm olive oil in a skillet over medium heat and cook garlic and red flakes for 2 minutes. Add in capers, anchovies, olives, salt, and pepper and cook for another 2-3 minutes until the anchovies melt into the oil. Blend tomatoes in a food processor. Pour into the skillet and stir-fry for 5 minutes. Mix in basil and pasta. Serve garnished with Parmesan cheese.

Nutrition Info:

- Info Per Serving: Calories: 443;Fat: 14g;Protein: 18g;Carbs: 65g.

Mediterranean Brown Rice

Servings:4
Cooking Time:20 Minutes
Ingredients:

- 1 lb asparagus, steamed and chopped
- 2 tbsp olive oil
- 3 tbsp balsamic vinegar
- 1 cup brown rice
- 2 tsp mustard
- Salt and black pepper to taste
- 5 oz baby spinach
- ½ cup parsley, chopped
- 1 tbsp tarragon, chopped

Directions:

1. Bring to a boil a pot of salted water over medium heat. Add in brown rice and cook for 7-9 minutes until al dente. Drain and place in a bowl. Add the asparagus to the same pot and blanch them for 4-5 minutes. Remove them to the rice bowl. Mix in spinach, olive oil, balsamic vinegar, mustard, salt, pepper, parsley, and tarragon. Serve.

Nutrition Info:

- Info Per Serving: Calories: 330;Fat: 12g;Protein: 11g;Carbs: 17g.

Mozzarella & Asparagus Pasta

Servings:6
Cooking Time:40 Minutes
Ingredients:

- 1 ½ lb asparagus, trimmed, cut into 1-inch
- 2 tbsp olive oil
- 8 oz orecchiette
- 2 cups cherry tomatoes, halved
- Salt and black pepper to taste
- 2 cups fresh mozzarella, drained and chopped
- ⅓ cup torn basil leaves
- 2 tbsp balsamic vinegar

Directions:

1. Preheat oven to 390 F. In a large pot, cook the pasta according to the directions. Drain, reserving ¼ cup of cooking water.

2. In the meantime, in a large bowl, toss in asparagus, cherry tomatoes, oil, pepper, and salt. Spread the mixture onto a rimmed baking sheet and bake for 15 minutes, stirring twice throughout cooking. Remove the veggies from the oven, and add the cooked pasta to the baking sheet. Mix with a few tbsp of pasta water to smooth the sauce and veggies. Slowly mix in the mozzarella and basil. Drizzle with the balsamic vinegar and serve in bowls.

Nutrition Info:

- Info Per Serving: Calories: 188;Fat: 11g;Protein: 14g;Carbs: 23g.

Kale & Feta Couscous

Servings:4
Cooking Time:20 Minutes
Ingredients:

- 2 tbsp olive oil
- 1 cup couscous
- 1 cup kale, chopped
- 1 tbsp parsley, chopped
- 3 spring onions, chopped
- 1 cucumber, chopped
- 1 tsp allspice
- ½ lemon, juiced and zested
- 4 oz feta cheese, crumbled

Directions:

1. In a bowl, place couscous and cover with hot water. Let sit for 10 minutes and fluff. Warm the olive oil in a skillet over medium heat and sauté onions and allspice for 3 minutes. Stir in the remaining ingredients and cook for 5-6 minutes.

Nutrition Info:

- Info Per Serving: Calories: 210;Fat: 7g;Protein: 5g;Carbs: 16g.

Quinoa With Baby Potatoes And Broccoli

Servings:4

Cooking Time: 10 Minutes

Ingredients:

- 2 tablespoons olive oil
- 1 cup baby potatoes, cut in half
- 1 cup broccoli florets
- 2 cups cooked quinoa
- Zest of 1 lemon
- Sea salt and freshly ground pepper, to taste

Directions:

1. Heat the olive oil in a large skillet over medium heat until shimmering.
2. Add the potatoes and cook for about 6 to 7 minutes, or until softened and golden brown. Add the broccoli and cook for about 3 minutes, or until tender.
3. Remove from the heat and add the quinoa and lemon zest. Season with salt and pepper to taste, then serve.

Nutrition Info:

- Info Per Serving: Calories: 205;Fat: 8.6g;Protein: 5.1g;Carbs: 27.3g.

Eggplant & Chickpea Casserole

Servings:6

Cooking Time:75 Minutes

Ingredients:

- ¼ cup olive oil
- 2 onions, chopped
- 1 green bell pepper, chopped
- Salt and black pepper to taste
- 3 garlic cloves, minced
- 1 tsp dried oregano
- ½ tsp ground cumin
- 1 lb eggplants, cubed
- 1 can tomatoes, diced
- 2 cans chickpeas

Directions:

1. Preheat oven to 400 F. Warm the olive oil in a skillet over medium heat. Add the onions, bell pepper, salt, and pepper.
2. Cook for about 5 minutes until softened. Stir in garlic, oregano, and cumin for about 30 seconds until fragrant. Transfer to a baking dish and add the eggplants, tomatoes, and chickpeas and stir. Place in the oven and bake for 45-60 minutes, shaking the dish twice during cooking. Serve.

Nutrition Info:

- Info Per Serving: Calories: 260;Fat: 12g;Protein: 8g;Carbs: 33.4g.

Chickpea & Couscous With Apricots

Servings:4
Cooking Time:30 Minutes
Ingredients:

- 2 tbsp olive oil
- 1 red onion, chopped
- 2 garlic cloves, minced
- 14 oz canned chickpeas
- 2 cups veggie stock
- 2 cups couscous, cooked
- ½ cup dried apricots, chopped
- Salt and black pepper to taste

Directions:

1. Warm the olive oil in a skillet over medium heat and cook onion and garlic for 5 minutes. Put in chickpeas, stock, apricots, salt, and pepper and cook for 15 minutes. Ladle couscous into bowls. Top with chickpea mixture.

Nutrition Info:

- Info Per Serving: Calories: 270;Fat: 12g;Protein: 8g;Carbs: 23g.

Catalan Sherry Fennel Millet

Servings:6
Cooking Time:40 Minutes
Ingredients:

- 1 fennel bulb, stalks discarded, cored, and finely chopped
- 3 tbsp olive oil
- 1 ½ cups millet
- Salt and black pepper to taste
- 1 onion, chopped fine
- 3 garlic cloves, minced
- ¼ tsp dried thyme
- 1 oz Parmesan cheese, grated
- ¼ cup minced fresh parsley
- 2 tsp sherry vinegar

Directions:

1. Bring 4 quarts of salted water to boil in a pot. Add millet and cook until tender, 15-20 minutes. Drain millet, return to now-empty pot, and cover to keep warm.
2. Heat 2 tablespoons oil in a skillet over medium heat until shimmering. Add onion, fennel, and salt and cook, stirring occasionally, until softened, 8-10 minutes. Add garlic and thyme and cook until fragrant, 30 seconds. Add the remaining oil and millet and cook, stirring frequently until heated through, 2 minutes. Off heat, stir in Parmesan, parsley, and vinegar. Season with salt and pepper to taste.

Nutrition Info:

- Info Per Serving: Calories: 312;Fat: 16g;Protein: 11g;Carbs: 29g.

Fruits, Desserts And Snacks Recipes

Lemony Tea And Chia Pudding

Servings:3
Cooking Time: 0 Minutes
Ingredients:

- 2 teaspoons matcha green tea powder (optional)
- 2 tablespoons ground chia seeds
- 1 to 2 dates
- 2 cups unsweetened coconut milk
- Zest and juice of 1 lime

Directions:

1. Put all the ingredients in a food processor and pulse until creamy and smooth.
2. Pour the mixture in a bowl, then wrap in plastic. Store in the refrigerator for at least 20 minutes, then serve chilled.

Nutrition Info:

- Info Per Serving: Calories: 225;Fat: 20.1g;Protein: 3.2g;Carbs: 5.9g.

Anchovy Stuffed Avocado Boats

Servings:4
Cooking Time:10 Minutes
Ingredients:

- 4 anchovy fillets, chopped
- 1 avocado, halved and pitted
- 2 tbsp sun-dried tomatoes, chopped
- 1 tbsp basil pesto
- 2 tbsp black olives, pitted and chopped
- Salt and black pepper to taste
- 2 tsp pine nuts, toasted
- 1 tbsp basil, chopped

Directions:

1. Toss anchovies, sun-dried tomatoes, basil pesto, olives, salt, pepper, pine nuts, and basil in a bowl. Fill each avocado half with the mixture and serve immediately.

Nutrition Info:

- Info Per Serving: Calories: 240;Fat: 10g;Protein: 6g;Carbs: 12g.

Spiced Fries

Servings:6
Cooking Time:35 Minutes
Ingredients:

- 2 lb red potatoes, cut into wedges
- ¼ cup olive oil
- 3 tbsp garlic, minced
- ½ tsp smoked paprika
- Salt and black pepper to taste
- ½ cup fresh cilantro, chopped
- ¼ tsp cayenne pepper

Directions:

1. Preheat oven to 450 F. Place the potatoes into a bowl. Add the garlic, salt, pepper, and olive oil and toss everything together to coat evenly. Spread the potato mixture onto a baking sheet; bake for 25 minutes, flipping them halfway through the cooking time until golden and crisp. Sprinkle the potatoes with cilantro, cayenne pepper, and smoked paprika. Serve warm and enjoy!

Nutrition Info:

- Info Per Serving: Calories: 203;Fat: 11g;Protein: 3g;Carbs: 24g.

Prawn & Cucumber Bites

Servings:4
Cooking Time:5 Minutes
Ingredients:

- 1 lb prawns, cooked and chopped
- 1 cucumber, cubed
- 2 tbsp cream cheese
- Salt and black pepper to taste
- 12 whole-grain crackers

Directions:

1. Combine cucumber, prawns, cream cheese, salt, and pepper in a bowl. Place crackers on a plate and top them with the prawn mixture. Serve right away.

Nutrition Info:

- Info Per Serving: Calories: 160;Fat: 9g;Protein: 18g;Carbs: 12g.

Chive Ricotta Spread

Servings:4
Cooking Time:5 Minutes
Ingredients:

- 2 tbsp extra virgin olive oil
- 8 oz ricotta cheese, crumbled
- 2 tbsp fresh parsley, chopped
- ¼ cup chives, chopped
- Salt and black pepper to taste

Directions:

1. In a blender, pulse ricotta cheese, parsley, chives, salt, pepper, and olive oil until smooth. Serve.

Nutrition Info:

- Info Per Serving: Calories: 260;Fat: 12g;Protein: 12g;Carbs: 9g.

Crispy Potato Chips

Servings:4
Cooking Time:40 Minutes
Ingredients:

- 2 tbsp olive oil
- 4 potatoes, cut into wedges
- 2 tbsp grated Parmesan cheese
- Salt and black pepper to taste

Directions:

1. Preheat the oven to 340 F. In a bowl, combine the potatoes, olive oil, salt, and black pepper. Spread on a lined baking sheet and bake for 40 minutes until the edges are browned. Serve sprinkled with Parmesan cheese.

Nutrition Info:

- Info Per Serving: Calories: 359;Fat: 8g;Protein: 9g;Carbs: 66g.

Grilled Peaches With Whipped Ricotta

Servings:4

Cooking Time: 14 To 22 Minutes

Ingredients:

- 4 peaches, halved and pitted
- 2 teaspoons extra-virgin olive oil
- ¾ cup whole-milk Ricotta cheese
- 1 tablespoon honey
- ¼ teaspoon freshly grated nutmeg
- 4 sprigs mint
- Cooking spray

Directions:

1. Spritz a grill pan with cooking spray. Heat the grill pan to medium heat.
2. Place a large, empty bowl in the refrigerator to chill.
3. Brush the peaches all over with the oil. Place half of the peaches, cut-side down, on the grill pan and cook for 3 to 5 minutes, or until grill marks appear.
4. Using tongs, turn the peaches over. Cover the grill pan with aluminum foil and cook for 4 to 6 minutes, or until the peaches are easily pierced with a sharp knife. Set aside to cool. Repeat with the remaining peaches.
5. Remove the bowl from the refrigerator and add the Ricotta. Using an electric beater, beat the Ricotta on high for 2 minutes. Add the honey and nutmeg and beat for 1 more minute.
6. Divide the cooled peaches among 4 serving bowls. Top with the Ricotta mixture and a sprig of mint and serve.

Nutrition Info:

- Info Per Serving: Calories: 176;Fat: 8.0g;Protein: 8.0g;Carbs: 20.0g.

Raspberry Yogurt Basted Cantaloupe

Servings:6

Cooking Time: 0 Minutes

Ingredients:

- 2 cups fresh raspberries, mashed
- 1 cup plain coconut yogurt
- ½ teaspoon vanilla extract
- 1 cantaloupe, peeled and sliced
- ½ cup toasted coconut flakes

Directions:

1. Combine the mashed raspberries with yogurt and vanilla extract in a small bowl. Stir to mix well.
2. Place the cantaloupe slices on a platter, then top with raspberry mixture and spread with toasted coconut.
3. Serve immediately.

Nutrition Info:

- Info Per Serving: Calories: 75;Fat: 4.1g;Protein: 1.2g;Carbs: 10.9g.

Mint-watermelon Gelato

Servings:4

Cooking Time:10 Min + Freezing Time

Ingredients:

- ¼ cup honey
- 4 cups watermelon cubes
- ¼ cup lemon juice
- 12 mint leaves to serve

Directions:

1. In a food processor, blend the watermelon, honey, and lemon juice to form a purée with chunks. Transfer to a freezer-proof container and place in the freezer for 1 hour.
2. Remove the container from and scrape with a fork. Return the to the freezer and repeat the process every half hour until the sorbet is completely frozen, for around 4 hours. Share into bowls, garnish with mint leaves, and serve.

Nutrition Info:

- Info Per Serving: Calories: 149;Fat: 0.4g;Protein: 1.8g;Carbs: 38g.

Savory Cauliflower Steaks

Servings:4
Cooking Time:35 Minutes
Ingredients:

- 1 head cauliflower, cut into steaks
- 2 tbsp olive oil
- Salt and paprika to taste

Directions:

1. Preheat oven to 360 F.Line a baking sheet with aluminum foil. Rub each cauliflower steak with olive oil, salt, and paprika. Arrange on the baking sheet and bake for 10-15 minutes, flip, and bake for another 15 minutes until crispy.

Nutrition Info:

- Info Per Serving: Calories: 78;Fat: 7g;Protein: 1g;Carbs: 4g.

Baked Zucchini Boats Stuffed With Feta

Servings:4
Cooking Time:50 Minutes
Ingredients:

- 2 zucchinis, halved lengthwise
- 2 tbsp olive oil
- 1 egg
- 2 garlic cloves, minced
- 2 tbsp oregano, chopped
- Salt and black pepper to taste
- 1 cup feta cheese, crumbled

Directions:

1. Preheat the oven to 390 F. Line a baking sheet with parchment paper. Scoop the flesh from the zucchini halves to make shells and place them on the baking sheet. In a bowl, mix egg, feta cheese, garlic, oregano, salt, pepper, and olive oil and bake for 40 minutes. Remove to a plate and serve.

Nutrition Info:

- Info Per Serving: Calories: 200;Fat: 16.5g;Protein: 8.3g;Carbs: 7g.

Bean & Artichoke Dip

Servings:4
Cooking Time:10 Minutes
Ingredients:

- 2 tbsp olive oil
- 15 oz canned Cannellini beans
- 1 red onion, chopped
- 6 oz canned artichoke hearts,
- 4 garlic cloves, minced
- 1 tbsp thyme, chopped
- ½ lemon, juiced and zested
- Salt and black pepper to taste

Directions:

1. Warm olive oil in a skillet over medium heat and sauté onion and garlic for 4-5 minutes until translucent. Add in the artichoke hearts and cook for 2-3 more minutes. Set aside to cool slightly. Transfer the cooled mixture to a blender along with cannellini beans, thyme, lemon juice, lemon zest, salt, and pepper and blitz until it becomes smooth. Serve.

Nutrition Info:

- Info Per Serving: Calories: 280;Fat: 12g;Protein: 17g;Carbs: 19g.

Choco-tahini Glazed Apple Chips

Servings:2
Cooking Time:10 Minutes
Ingredients:

- 1 tbsp roasted, salted sunflower seeds
- 2 tbsp tahini
- 1 tbsp honey
- 1 tbsp cocoa powder
- 2 apples, thinly sliced

Directions:

1. Mix the tahini, honey, and cocoa powder in a small bowl. Add 1-2 tbsp of warm water and stir until thin enough to drizzle. Lay the apple chips out on a plate and drizzle them with the chocolate tahini sauce. Sprinkle sunflower seeds.

Nutrition Info:

- Info Per Serving: Calories: 261;Fat: 11g;Protein: 5g;Carbs: 43g.

Spiced Nut Mix

Servings:6
Cooking Time:20 Minutes
Ingredients:

- 1 tbsp olive oil
- 2 cups raw mixed nuts
- 1 tsp ground cumin
- ½ tsp garlic powder
- ½ tsp kosher salt
- ⅛ tsp chili powder
- ⅛ tsp ground coriander

Directions:

1. Place the nuts in a skillet over medium heat and toast for 3 minutes, shaking the pan continuously. Remove to a bowl, season with salt, and reserve. Warm olive oil in the same skillet. Add in cumin, garlic powder, chili powder, and ground coriander and cook for about 20-30 seconds. Mix in nuts and cook for another 4 minutes. Serve chilled.

Nutrition Info:

- Info Per Serving: Calories: 315;Fat: 29.2g;Protein: 8g;Carbs: 11g.

Vegetarian Patties

Servings:4
Cooking Time:20 Minutes
Ingredients:

- 3 tbsp olive oil
- 2 carrots, grated
- 2 zucchinis, grated and drained
- 2 garlic cloves, minced
- 2 spring onions, chopped
- 1 tsp cumin
- ½ tsp turmeric powder
- Salt and black pepper to taste
- ¼ tsp ground coriander
- 2 tbsp parsley, chopped
- ¼ tsp lemon juice
- ½ cup flour
- 1 egg, whisked
- ¼ cup breadcrumbs

Directions:

1. Combine garlic, spring onions, carrot, cumin, turmeric, salt, pepper, coriander, parsley, lemon juice, flour, zucchinis, egg, and breadcrumbs in a bowl and mix well. Form balls out of the mixture and flatten them to form patties.
2. Warm olive oil in a skillet over medium heat. Fry the cakes for 10 minutes on both sides. Remove to a paper-lined plate to drain the excessive grease. Serve warm.

Nutrition Info:

- Info Per Serving: Calories: 220;Fat: 12g;Protein: 5g;Carbs: 5g.

Avocado & Dark Chocolate Mousse

Servings:4
Cooking Time:10 Min + Freezing Time
Ingredients:
- 2 tbsp olive oil
- 8 oz dark chocolate, chopped
- ¼ cup milk
- 2 ripe avocados, deseeded
- ¼ cup honey
- 1 cup strawberries

Directions:
1. Cook the chocolate, olive oil, and milk in a saucepan over medium heat for 3 minutes or until the chocolate melt, stirring constantly. Put the avocado in a food processor, then drizzle with honey and melted chocolate. Pulse to combine until smooth. Pour the mixture into a serving bowl, then sprinkle with strawberries. Chill for 30 minutes and serve.

Nutrition Info:
- Info Per Serving: Calories: 654;Fat: 47g;Protein: 7.2g;Carbs: 56g.

No-gluten Caprese Pizza

Servings:4
Cooking Time:40 Minutes
Ingredients:
- 2 tbsp olive oil
- 2 ¼ cups chickpea flour
- Salt and black pepper to taste
- 1 tsp onion powder
- 1 tomato, sliced
- ¼ tsp dried oregano
- 2 oz mozzarella cheese, sliced
- ¼ cup tomato sauce
- 2 tbsp fresh basil, chopped

Directions:
1. Preheat oven to 360 F. Combine the chickpea flour, salt, pepper, 1 ¼ cups of water, olive oil, and onion powder in a bowl. Mix well to form a soft dough, then knead a bit until elastic. Let sit covered in a greased bowl to rise, for 25 minutes in a warm place. Remove the dough to a floured surface and roll out it with a rolling pin into a thin circle.
2. Transfer to a floured baking tray and bake in the oven for 10 minutes. Evenly spread the tomato sauce over the pizza base. Sprinkle with oregano and arrange the mozzarella cheese and tomato slices on top. Bake for 10 minutes. Top with basil and serve sliced.

Nutrition Info:
- Info Per Serving: Calories: 420;Fat: 26g;Protein: 14g;Carbs: 35g.

Thyme Lentil Spread

Servings:6
Cooking Time:10 Minutes
Ingredients:
- 3 tbsp olive oil
- 1 garlic clove, minced
- 1 cup split red lentils, rinsed
- ½ tsp dried thyme
- 1 tbsp balsamic vinegar
- Salt and black pepper to taste

Directions:
1. Bring to a boil salted water in a pot over medium heat. Add in the lentils and cook for 15 minutes until cooked through. Drain and set aside to cool. In a food processor, place the lentils, garlic, thyme, vinegar, salt, and pepper. Gradually add olive oil while blending until smooth. Serve.

Nutrition Info:
- Info Per Serving: Calories: 295;Fat: 10g;Protein: 10g;Carbs: 16g.

White Bean Dip The Greek Way

Servings:6

Cooking Time:5 Minutes

Ingredients:

- ¼ cup extra-virgin olive oil
- 1 lemon, zested and juiced
- 1 can white beans
- 2 garlic cloves, minced
- ¼ tsp ground cumin
- 2 tbsp Greek oregano, chopped
- 1 tsp stone-ground mustard
- Salt to taste

Directions:

1. In a food processor, blend all the ingredients, except for the oregano, until smooth. Top with Greek oregano and serve.

Nutrition Info:

- Info Per Serving: Calories: 222;Fat: 7g;Protein: 12g;Carbs: 30.4g.

Baked Balsamic Beet Rounds

Servings:6

Cooking Time:45 Minutes

Ingredients:

- 4 tbsp olive oil
- 4 beets, peeled, cut into wedges
- Salt and black pepper to taste
- 3 tsp fresh thyme
- ⅓ cup balsamic vinegar
- 1 tbsp fresh dill, chopped

Directions:

1. Preheat oven to 400 F. Place the beets into a large bowl. Add 2 tbsp of olive oil, salt, and thyme and toss to combine. Spread the beets onto a baking sheet. Bake for 35-40 minutes, turning once or twice until the beets are tender. Remove and let them cool for 10 minutes. In a small bowl, whisk together the remaining olive oil, vinegar, dill, and black pepper. Transfer the beets into a serving bowl, spoon the vinegar mixture over the beets, and serve.

Nutrition Info:

- Info Per Serving: Calories: 111;Fat: 7g;Protein: 2g;Carbs: 11g.

Frozen Mango Raspberry Delight

Servings:2

Cooking Time: 0 Minutes

Ingredients:

- 3 cups frozen raspberries
- 1 mango, peeled and pitted
- 1 peach, peeled and pitted
- 1 teaspoon honey

Directions:

1. Place all the ingredients into a blender and purée, adding some water as needed.
2. Put in the freezer for 10 minutes to firm up if desired. Serve chilled or at room temperature.

Nutrition Info:

- Info Per Serving: Calories: 276;Fat: 2.1g;Protein: 4.5g;Carbs: 60.3g.

Walnut And Date Balls

Servings:6
Cooking Time: 8 To 10 Minutes
Ingredients:
- 1 cup walnuts
- 1 cup unsweetened shredded coconut
- 14 medjool dates, pitted
- 8 tablespoons almond butter

Directions:
1. Preheat the oven to 350°F.
2. Put the walnuts on a baking sheet and toast in the oven for 5 minutes.
3. Put the shredded coconut on a clean baking sheet. Toast for about 3 to 5 minutes, or until it turns golden brown. Once done, remove it from the oven and put it in a shallow bowl.
4. In a food processor, process the toasted walnuts until they have a medium chop. Transfer the chopped walnuts into a medium bowl.
5. Add the dates and butter to the food processor and blend until the dates become a thick paste. Pour the chopped walnuts into the food processor with the dates and pulse just until the mixture is combined, about 5 to 7 pulses.
6. Remove the mixture from the food processor and scrape it into a large bowl.
7. To make the balls, spoon 1 to 2 tablespoons of the date mixture into the palm of your hand and roll around between your hands until you form a ball. Put the ball on a clean, lined baking sheet. Repeat until all the mixture is formed into balls.
8. Roll each ball in the toasted coconut until the outside of the ball is coated. Put the ball back on the baking sheet and repeat.
9. Put all the balls into the refrigerator for 20 minutes before serving. Store any leftovers in the refrigerator in an airtight container.

Nutrition Info:
- Info Per Serving: Calories: 489;Fat: 35.0g;Protein: 5.0g;Carbs: 48.0g.

Banana, Cranberry, And Oat Bars

Servings:16
Cooking Time: 40 Minutes
Ingredients:
- 2 tablespoon extra-virgin olive oil
- 2 medium ripe bananas, mashed
- ½ cup almond butter
- ½ cup maple syrup
- ⅓ cup dried cranberries
- 1½ cups old-fashioned rolled oats
- ¼ cup oat flour
- ¼ cup ground flaxseed
- ¼ teaspoon ground cloves
- ½ cup shredded coconut
- ½ teaspoon ground cinnamon
- 1 teaspoon vanilla extract

Directions:
1. Preheat the oven to 400°F. Line a 8-inch square pan with parchment paper, then grease with olive oil.
2. Combine the mashed bananas, almond butter, and maple syrup in a bowl. Stir to mix well.
3. Mix in the remaining ingredients and stir to mix well until thick and sticky.
4. Spread the mixture evenly on the square pan with a spatula, then bake in the preheated oven for 40 minutes or until a toothpick inserted in the center comes out clean.
5. Remove them from the oven and slice into 16 bars to serve.

Nutrition Info:
- Info Per Serving: Calories: 145;Fat: 7.2g;Protein: 3.1g;Carbs: 18.9g.

Italian Popcorn

Servings:6
Cooking Time:20 Minutes
Ingredients:

- 2 tbsp butter, melted
- 1 tbsp truffle oil
- 8 cups air-popped popcorn
- 2 tbsp packed brown sugar
- 2 tbsp Italian seasoning
- ¼ tsp sea salt

Directions:

1. Preheat oven to 350 F. Combine butter, Italian seasoning, sugar, and salt in a bowl. Pour over the popcorn and toss well to coat. Remove to a baking dish and bake for 15 minutes, stirring frequently. Drizzle with truffle oil and serve.

Nutrition Info:

- Info Per Serving: Calories: 80;Fat: 5g;Protein: 1.1g;Carbs: 8.4g.

Speedy Granita

Servings:4
Cooking Time:10 Min + Freezing Time
Ingredients:

- ¼ cup sugar
- 1 cup fresh strawberries
- 1 cup fresh raspberries
- 1 cup chopped fresh kiwi
- 1 tsp lemon juice

Directions:

1. Bring 1 cup water to a boil in a small saucepan over high heat. Add the sugar and stir well until dissolved. Remove the pan from the heat, add the fruit and lemon juice, and cool to room temperature. Once cooled, puree the fruit in a blender until smooth. Pour the puree into a shallow glass baking dish and place in the freezer for 1 hour. Stir with a fork and freeze for 30 minutes, then repeat. Serve and enjoy!

Nutrition Info:

- Info Per Serving: Calories: 153;Fat: 0.2g;Protein: 1.6g;Carbs: 39g.

Spanish Cheese Crackers

Servings:6
Cooking Time:20 Min + Chilling Time
Ingredients:

- 4 tbsp butter, softened
- 1 cup Manchego cheese, grated
- 1 cup flour
- ¼ tsp dried tarragon
- Salt and black pepper to taste
- 1 large egg

Directions:

1. With an electric mixer, cream together the butter and shredded cheese until well combined and smooth. In a small bowl, combine the flour, salt, and pepper. Gradually add the flour mixture to the cheese, mixing constantly until the dough forms a ball. Wrap tightly with plastic wrap and refrigerate for at least 1 hour.

2. Preheat oven to 350 F. In a small bowl, whisk together the egg with salt. Slice the refrigerated dough into small rounds, about ¼ inch thick, and place on two parchment-lined baking sheets. Brush the tops of the crackers with egg wash and bake until the crackers are golden and crispy, 12-15 minutes. Remove from the oven and allow to cool on a wire rack. Serve cooled.

Nutrition Info:

- Info Per Serving: Calories: 243;Fat: 23g;Protein: 8g;Carbs: 2g.

Appendix : Recipes Index

Chive Ricotta Spread 77
Choco-tahini Glazed Apple Chips 80
Citrus Chicken Wings 30
Citrus Salad With Kale And Fennel 63
Classic Shakshuka 14
Cream Peach Smoothie 12
Creamy Halibut & Potato Soup 19
Creamy Polenta With Mushrooms 49
Crispy Potato Chips 77
Cucumber Gazpacho 58
Cumin Quinoa Pilaf 71

D

Deluxe Chicken With Yogurt Sauce 38
Dragon Pork Chops With Pickle Topping 29
Drunken Lamb Bake 34

E

Easy Pork Stew 32
Easy Spring Salad 54
Eggplant & Chickpea Casserole 74
Eggplant & Turkey Moussaka 36
Eggplant, Spinach, And Feta Sandwiches 9

F

Fennel Beef Ribs 30
Feta & Zucchini Rosti Cakes 39
Fish & Chickpea Stew 48
Frozen Mango Raspberry Delight 82

G

Garbanzo & Arugula Salad With Blue Cheese 61
Garlic-butter Parmesan Salmon And Asparagus 17
Garlicky Zucchini Cubes With Mint 42
Gluten-free Almond-crusted Salmon 27
Greek-style Chickpea Salad 67
Green Veggie Sandwiches 15
Greens, Fennel, And Pear Soup With Cashews 56
Grilled Lemon Chicken 34
Grilled Peaches With Whipped Ricotta 78
Grilled Pork Chops With Apricot Chutney 33

H

Ham, Bean & Sweet Potato Frittata 14
Herby Artichoke Frittata With Ricotta 6
Hot Jumbo Shrimp 25
Hot Tomato & Caper Squid Stew 24
Hot Zucchini & Egg Nests 13

I

Israeli Couscous With Asparagus 65
Italian Popcorn 84

K

Kale & Feta Couscous 73
Kale-proscuitto Porridge 6

L

Lamb Tagine With Couscous And Almonds 35
Lazy Blueberry Oatmeal 11
Lebanese Crunchy Salad With Seeds 54
Lemon-garlic Sea Bass 17
Lemony Lamb Stew 55
Lemony Tea And Chia Pudding 76
Lentil And Mushroom Pasta 67

M

Mackerel & Radish Salad 60
Mediterranean Brown Rice 73
Mini Crustless Spinach Quiches 47
Mint & Lemon Cranberry Beans 64
Mint-watermelon Gelato 78
Morning Overnight Oats With Raspberries 10
Moroccan Rice Pilaf 68
Moroccan Spiced Couscous 59
Moroccan-style Vegetable Bean Stew 64
Moules Mariniere (mussels In Wine Sauce) 25
Mozzarella & Asparagus Pasta 73
Mushroom Filled Zucchini Boats 44

N

No-gluten Caprese Pizza 81
North African Grilled Fish Fillets 19
Nut & Plum Parfait 9
Nutty Chicken Breasts 31

O

Octopus, Calamari & Watercress Salad 61
Olive Tapenade Flatbread With Cheese 57
Orange-honey Glazed Carrots 55
Oregano Chicken Risotto 66

P

Pan-fried Chili Sea Scallops 22
Pan-fried Tuna With Vegetables 26
Paprika Cauliflower Steaks With Walnut Sauce 43
Parsley & Olive Zucchini Bake 50
Parsley Beef Fusilli 65
Parsley Eggplant Lamb 36
Parsley Halibut With Roasted Peppers 20
Parsley Littleneck Clams In Sherry Sauce 20
Pearl Barley Risotto With Parmesan Cheese 72
Pecorino Bulgur & Spinach Cupcakes 15
Pork Chop & Arugula Salad 59
Pork Millet With Chestnuts 38
Prawn & Cucumber Bites 77
Prawns With Mushrooms 17
Pumpkin Pie Parfait 13

Q

Quinoa With Baby Potatoes And Broccoli 74

R

Rainbow Vegetable Kebabs 45
Raspberry & Nut Quinoa 67
Raspberry Yogurt Basted Cantaloupe 78
Rice And Blueberry Stuffed Sweet Potatoes 66
Rich Chicken And Small Pasta Broth 58
Ricotta Muffins With Pear Glaze 12
Roasted Pepper & Tomato Soup 52
Roasted Red Pepper & Olive Spread 62
Roasted Red Snapper With Citrus Topping 18
Roasted Salmon With Tomatoes & Capers 22
Roasted Vegetables And Chickpeas 46
Roasted Veggies And Brown Rice Bowl 50

S

Salmon Salad Wraps 11
Savory Cauliflower Steaks 79
Scallion Clams With Snow Peas 27
Seared Salmon With Lemon Cream Sauce 18
Shrimp & Gnocchi With Feta Cheese 24
Simple Braised Carrots 46
Simple Chicken With Olive Tapenade 35
Skillet Eggplant & Kale Frittata 13
Slow Cooker Beef Stew 28
Spanish Cheese Crackers 84
Speedy Granita 84
Spiced Fries 76
Spiced Nut Mix 80
Spinach & Bean Salad With Goat Cheese 52
Spinach And Egg Breakfast Wraps 8

Spinach Chicken With Chickpeas 28
Stewed Chicken Sausage With Farro 37
Stuffed Portobello Mushrooms With Spinach 51

T

Tasty Chicken Pot 37
Tasty Lentil Burgers 40
The Ultimate Chicken Bean Soup 62
Three-bean Salad With Black Olives 56
Thyme Lentil Spread 81
Tomato & Basil Chicken Breasts 33
Tomato Basil Pasta 70
Tomato Bean & Sausage Casserole 69
Tomato Caper & Turkey Pot 31
Tomato Eggs With Fried Potatoes 12
Tomato Sauce And Basil Pesto Fettuccine 68
Tomato Seafood Soup 20
Traditional Mushroom Risotto 71
Traditional Tuscan Scallops 21
Tuna And Olive Salad Sandwiches 7
Tuna And Zucchini Patties 21
Tuscan-style Panzanella Salad 57

V

Vegan Lentil Bolognese 40
Vegetable & Hummus Bowl 10
Vegetarian Patties 80

W

Walnut And Date Balls 83
White Bean Dip The Greek Way 82
Wild Rice, Celery, And Cauliflower Pilaf 70
Wilted Dandelion Greens With Sweet Onion 45

Z

Zesty Spanish Potato Salad 59
Ziti Marinara Bake 69
Zoodles With Walnut Pesto 43

Printed in Great Britain
by Amazon

30176280R00057